HOW T(
A GUIDE FOR YOU   NTS

In this Series

How to Be an Effective School Governor
How to Buy & Run a Shop
How to Choose a Private School
How to Claim State Benefits
How to Do Your Own Advertising
How to Employ & Manage Staff
How to Enjoy Retirement
How to Get a Job Abroad
How to Get That Job
How to Help Your Child at School
How to Keep Business Accounts
How to Live & Work in America
How to Live & Work in Australia
How to Live & Work in France
How to Lose Weight & Keep Fit
How to Master Business English
How to Master Public Speaking
How to Pass Exams Without Anxiety
How to Plan a Wedding
How to Prepare Your Child for School
How to Raise Business Finance
How to Run a Local Campaign
How to Start a Business from Home
How to Study Abroad
How to Study & Live in Britain
How to Survive at College
How to Survive Divorce
How to Take Care of Your Heart
How to Teach Abroad
How to Use a Library
How to Write for Publication

other titles in preparation

How To Books

USE A LIBRARY

A GUIDE FOR YOUNG PEOPLE AND STUDENTS

Elizabeth King MA, ALA

Northcote House

© *1987 and 1990 by Elizabeth King.*

First published in 1987 by Northcote House Publishers Ltd,
Plymbridge House, Estover Road, Plymouth PL6 7PZ,
United Kingdom. Tel: Plymouth (0752) 705251. Telex: 45635. Fax: (0752) 777603.

Reprinted 1990.

All rights reserved. No part of this work may be reproduced other than
for the purposes of review without the express permission of the Publishers
given in writing.

British Library Cataloguing in Publication Data
King, Elizabeth
 How to use a library: a guide for young people and students.—(How to series)
 1. Library orientation—Great Britain
 I. Title
 025.5′6′0941   Z710

ISBN 0-7463-0317-3

Printed and bound in Great Britain by
BPCC Wheatons Ltd, Exeter

Contents

Introduction 6
1 Libraries are for You
    Who needs libraries? What is a library? Public libraries; school
    and college libraries; other libraries; spotting a good library 7
2 Your information supermarket 19
3 Using a library for study 25
4 Using books for reference 37
5 Using a library for research 43
6 Related sources
    Museums; newspapers; art galleries and picture libraries; press
    cuttings; record offices; church records; company records;
    Citizens Advice Bureaux; people as a resource 53
7 Special library services
    Telephone directories; electoral lists; local diary; tourist
    information; official leaflets and information; music and
    records; play and choir sets; video library; patents; exhibition
    collections; local history; large print books; teenage libraries;
    foreign language books; maps; illustration collections;
    photocopying; exam papers; computer programs; tapes,
    cassettes and educational videos; slides and filmstrips; Open
    University material; distance learning 61
8 The information revolution
    Computerised data bases; computer search; Prestel, Oracle
    and Ceefax 67
9 The librarian's day 75
10 Some important libraries in Britain
    The British Library; the national libraries of Wales and
    Scotland; Government libraries; the House of Commons
    library; charity organisation libraries; business libraries 85
Some useful addresses 89
Further reading 90
Glossary of terms 91
Index 95

INTRODUCTION

I hope this book will prove useful to *all* students, but particularly those tackling for the first time the challenge of finding their own information and sources. Teachers too may find it of help in promoting the more effective use of both libraries and study techniques.

This book owes much to my many friends for their help and support but especially to my daughter Alison, who also helped in the preparation of the manuscript, and to my son Richard.

ACKNOWLEDGEMENTS

All photographs appearing in this book (with the exception of the British Library Reading Room are reproduced with the kind permission of the County Librarian, Devon. The photograph on page 80 is reproduced with the permission of the British Library.

1
Libraries are for You

WHO NEEDS LIBRARIES?

Why have libraries? Well, think of some of the things you might need to find out in just one week.

1. The telephone number of a friend far away (you may not be too sure of the address, either).
2. More background on the French revolution for an important history essay.
3. How to get to the new disco — which bus?
4. How hot will it be in Majorca in July?
5. How do you make *chilli con carne*?
6. What on earth does EFL stand for?
7. What books has Frank Herbert written?
8. Which is the best compact disc system?
9. Where was great-grandfather born?
10. What's the address of the local athletics club?

If you live in a house with all books and no furniture, you might be able to find the answers to about three of these at home; all the rest would need access to a much larger collection of information. This might be either your school or college library, the local public library or perhaps even a specialised library dealing with only one subject like local history or food technology.

Without access to a library you — and thousands of other people — would be stuck! The amount of information you can carry around in your head, or buy to keep for yourself, is minute.

Information Supermarkets
That is the basic reason why libraries were set up in the first place, why they still exist today, and why they are not only getting bigger but also better able to respond to your needs and those of everyone else. Libraries are

important because they can hold vast storehouses of information which you, and anyone else, can tap into at any time. You can use a library for all the following and still not exhaust even half its possibilities:

- To find the answer to a simple question.
- To borrow something to read on a long journey.
- To learn a new skill.
- To help pass an exam.
- To discover new and unexpected information.
- As a place to study.

WHAT IS A LIBRARY?

Libraries are rather like liquorice allsorts. They come in all shapes and sizes but, like the sweets have the common denominator of 'liquorice', all libraries have the aim of collecting and then sharing information to everyone who needs it. Collections of information may be any of the following.

1. A dusty shelf in your bedroom filled with old comics, annuals, pop magazines and assorted paperbacks that you want to keep.
2. A musty collection in your elderly aunt's front room that is never touched.
3. A glass and concrete building full of high-tech machines, computer terminals and with a few books hidden away in a corner.
4. A shop down the road which once used to be the 'chippie', but is now your local branch library.
5. A shelf in a research worker's office with mainly highly specialised periodical articles.
6. A converted classroom in your school or college with perhaps homemade shelving and a book-stock that may vary from the very good to jumble sale cast-offs.
7. Miles and miles of shelving holding nearly all the books that have ever been written in English (like the British Museum Library in London).

These are all **libraries** of one sort or another and there are endless variations on this theme. But whatever their size, the common strand is a role as 'information providers'. Some libraries, like your own collection, may be 'private libraries': not anyone could just walk in off the street and borrow. However, just as you may be willing to lend books to your friends, so will some of these special libraries lend if you ask.

This sort of rule applies equally to your school or college library which has been primarily set up to help you and your fellow students. You can borrow automatically from that library but someone from another college would probably have to ask special permission.

Public libraries

Public libraries, though, are exactly what they say they are — open to anyone who lives or works in the area to borrow from, and open to anyone in the world who wants to look something up, read the latest issue of a magazine or just browse round the shelves. These libraries are paid for by the local rates, so no charge is made to local people who want to borrow books and only rarely for a particular service like a **record library**.

Let's look at some of the types of library you may find near to you.

Public Library

There is bound to be some sort of local public library service you can use, but a lot will depend on where you live as to what sort of library facilities you have. If you live or work in a big city then your library will probably be a very large central building with thousands of books, many different departments and scores of staff.

However, if you live in a small village or town or perhaps on the outskirts of a big city, much less may be on offer. It may be a small **branch library**, open for just a few hours per week, or a **mobile library** that only visits your village once a week.

"Can you tell me the way to Littleton Parva?"

But don't despair! — *every* public library service point (however small) is a link in a chain to *all* the books and resources available throughout all that library service, and from there to all other libraries and their stocks.

If you want to join the public library, you will probably be asked to fill in a simple form but unless you keep the books too long, lose them or let the dog chew them, it will cost you nothing at all. The only charge that may be made is if you want to borrow videos, records or things like that, but even this varies from area to area.

School and college libraries

Wherever you are studying you should find a library. It will vary depending on the size of your college and the subjects studied there. The chances are that if you are in college you will have a better library than at school. The reasons for this are complex, but like most things it comes down to money and staff. Colleges usually do better than schools in providing resources and, even more importantly, the library staff to run them and help you.

All educational establishments now realise the importance of a good library. In fact it is often one of the key points looked at by the examination boards when they decide which college should offer which subjects. A strong library is at the centre of all good education. However, you will probably have to make the best of what is on offer, but it is well worth knowing what else exists in your area that may help you. Even if your own library is very good, remember that everyone else on your course probably wants the same books, so if you have an alternative source up your sleeve, you'll be off to a head start.

Other colleges, polytechnics and universities

It is well worth finding out what other academic libraries there are near to you. They may not be happy to let you *borrow* (after all they have their own students to consider) but some will let you browse, read or study there. Since many of the larger ones are open for very long hours (sometimes on Sundays) they can be very useful places to know about.

Local firms

These often have specialised libraries run for the benefit of their staff — particularly any involved in research. The chances are that you will find really specialised resources and expert advice here. If any local large firms have links with your subject then take time and trouble to discover what they may have. If you are not sure what firms may be in your area, either check the yellow pages of the phone book or ask in your main public library. Your school or college librarian should also be a good source of local knowledge.

Careers Office

All large towns have a careers office. These exist not only to help people choose their future careers but also to keep information on job opportunities, local firms, sponsorship schemes and lots of other 'job' or education-related topics. One of the responsibilities of the careers office is to liaise with local industry, so they could tell you what else exists nearby.

Hospitals and other medical institutions
Doctors, nurses and all other paramedical staff have many pressing information needs, so all big hospitals have their own libraries. If it is a teaching hospital (where doctors and nurses are trained), then the stock will be that much bigger. You may not be able to borrow, but if you have any genuine enquiries the staff will almost certainly try and help you.

Local newspapers
All papers, however small and local, keep extensive records about the community they serve. These may be historical, to do with old buildings (including photos or illustrations), biographical information about noteworthy residents, or records of the ups and downs of local firms. You will always find old copies of newspapers in local newspaper libraries and, in the larger ones, probably a useful collection of press cuttings. The big national dailies such as *The Times* and *The Guardian* have extensive libraries with specialist library staff. They run an extremely efficient **current affairs information service** as well as providing background information for articles about everything under the sun.

Research establishments
Dotted around the country are all sorts of research institutions. Many of these are government backed and funded; all have specialised library staff to serve the needs of the research workers. Examples of the official type are **The Royal Greenwich Observatory** and the **Atlas Computer Laboratory**. Other establishments are set up and funded by the industries themselves; examples of these are the **Wool Industry Research Association** in Yorkshire and the **Rubber and Plastic Research Association** near Shrewsbury. These latter places often do research work on contract for industrial or official bodies but because they are all, of whatever type, working on the frontiers of new knowledge, they have very extensive and sophisticated information services. If what you are studying is *very* specialised, then it could well be worth your while approaching one of these.

Local societies
These are well worth a try. Many of them are long-established and have records stretching way back. Some of the bigger ones even have their own library and can offer all sorts of information within their own subject area. To find out what there may be near to you, ask at the public library. They should be able to tell you not only what societies exist in the area but also the name, address and telephone number of the secretary.

Other libraries

National libraries and collections
If you are lucky enough to live in London, Edinburgh or Aberystwyth, then you have a **National Library** right on your door-step. These are truly massive collections of all that has been published over the centuries in English (and many other languages as well). Their main function is as a **repository** to collect, keep and store material for all time.

They rarely lend anything and often make quite severe restrictions on who may use the study facilities. But if you get the chance, they are fascinating places to visit. London, in particular, also has lots of other major collections, often run in conjunction with the national museums, but their main use will always be reserved for the specialist research worker and the sorts of materials you need should usually be obtainable elsewhere.

> *The British Library Reading Room,*
> Great Russell Street, London WC1B 3DG.
>
> *The National Library of Scotland,*
> George IV Bridge, Edinburgh.
>
> *The National Library of Wales,*
> Aberystwyth, Dyfed SY23 3BU.

The Library network
This is not an individual library, but the means by which anyone anywhere can borrow books not readily available locally. Suppose you live in an isolated part of the country, or are unlucky in having a not very good library service; if you have exhausted all your local possibilities and still have not found what you need, do not despair. Throughout the country there is the **interloan** network set up to cope with just this problem. No one library can hold everything and sooner or later there will be something you need that is not in stock locally.

Arrangements will be made to borrow this from another library and in extreme cases books even come from libraries abroad. You may be asked to pay the postage for a book from another library but all the necessary paperwork will be done by the library. Your only job is to give the library full details of the book you need. If it is an article from a periodical, then you will probably be given a photocopy of the article to keep. Research workers find this particularly useful as it means they have continuing access to their information banks.

> ● *Tip* Never be afraid to approach any library anywhere. Most librarians are more than happy to share their knowledge and resources with all interested enquirers. It's always worth asking.

HOW TO SPOT A GOOD LIBRARY

Feeling at home
Do you feel at home there? Not always easy, as some libraries are still housed in old Victorian buildings which in themselves can sometimes be dark, gloomy and forbidding places. Even the staff in these places can feel their strait-laced predecessors frowning down on them. If your 'local' is like this, don't be too hard on the staff! Whatever the building, you should find the staff helpful and the atmosphere friendly. Do feel you can ask for any information — however simple — at any time.

Be yourself
You should feel relaxed and at home. If you do not know where to find what you want, or are not even sure what you do want, feel free to ask the staff without feeling you are losing face.

Finding your way around
The way the library is organised should help, not hinder you, to find your way around the shelves. Are there lots of notices, signs, shelf labels, guides on the actual shelves? Next time you go to a supermarket, look at *their* sign-posting. Does your library do as well?

A cared-for place
Does it look as though someone loves the library? Look for this wherever you go — school, hospital, library or whatever. Is it reasonably tidy but not *so* immaculate that you dare not touch anything? Are there plants, pictures, and helpful notices around the place? (Beware of the peeling yellow sellotape syndrome half holding up old notices!) If you are lucky enough to be in a library which is loved then you can be sure to find welcoming staff as well.

Rules and regulations

These should be minimal and positive rather than negative. Beware of libraries with DO NOT notices but look for ones that start PLEASE DO. There are always borrowers who ignore overdues, scribble in library books, and are generally a pain in the neck for both the library staff and the other users, so there must be *some* rules. However, these should be kept to a minimum and clearly explained so that everyone understands why they are important.

Services

Does the library make you aware of all the services it offers? How are you expected to know, for example, that you can borrow books from other libraries or perhaps have a **computer search** done if the library does not advertise these?

Displays and exhibitions

Most libraries, of whatever sort, will usually have some books on display. These may be a selection of their most recent purchases or, particularly if you are in a school or college library, on a theme or topic that is on the curriculum. These displays can often tell you a lot about the library, from basic information on the sort of new books they buy to an appreciation, in a school or college library, of how involved the library is in the academic work.

A good display will always bring together unusual and stimulating items that might otherwise be overlooked and they can highlight particular aspects of a subject. Other material, whether on video, cassette or computer program, may be included as well as perhaps actual artefacts.

> ● *Tip* Every environment is full of hidden clues about itself. Learn what you can about your library from the way it presents itself to you.

Staff

Can you find the staff when you need them, or are they always in a huddle in the workroom? Is there any clue as to which member of staff you should ask?

Library staff come in two distinct sorts although there is no way you can tell by looking. **Professional librarians** will have gone through at least three years of professional education and will be graduates in librarianship. Many of them, particularly in the universities, polytechnics and colleges, will have taken a degree in a special subject and then done a year of post-graduate librarianship education. This is a similar route to that taken by many teachers — the split coming when they decide which option to choose after their initial degree.

Professional librarians manage the library and its assistant staff. They help to select resources, provide special help for borrowers, compile book-lists and bibliographies, are expert in searching computer data bases and provide the vital link between the borrower and the appropriate information source. They are also heavily involved in the more technical library skills of classification, cataloguing and indexing — much of which now demands an ability and willingness to work with computers and other automated retrieval systems.

In college libraries one of the prime functions of the librarian is to liaise with the teaching staff to make sure that the library stock accurately reflects the various courses of study. He/she is also actively involved in teaching programmes of library and study skills to all students. Librarians are an important part of many college committees — particularly those that manage the college's resources and those that consider new courses.

Library assistants are the other sort of staff you will find. Their role is really to do all the house-keeping functions. They usually have no formal library qualifications; they look after the borrowing and return of books,

---

WANTED: LIBRARY ASSISTANT
Must be strong, agile, knowledgeable and nimble-fingered.

---

do the shelving and keep the books in order. Because of these tasks they are often very knowledgeable about what is on the shelves, and they can be of great help if you cannot find what you want. They also are responsible for other jobs like chasing up overdue books, repairing and labelling, and doing most of the typing and clerical work. In some small libraries there may be no qualified librarians but only library assistants.

● *Tip* Don't forget: the priority for all library staff is to *help their readers*. Never be afraid to ask or interrupt their back-room work.

If you live in or near a large city, then your public library will probably be split into different departments. This is rather like a large store separating men's from children's wear or carpets from electrical, but it can be a little confusing unless you have some idea of what to expect. Some libraries are not as good as others at telling you not only *what* they have but also *where* to find it.

Most of the big libraries will have some or all of the following but don't be confused if they call them something slightly different.

Library departments

Department	Description
Lending Library	Usually one of the biggest departments with both fiction and non-fiction, all of which can be borrowed. Emphasis on **recreational** reading rather than material for the serious student. However, do not dismiss these books out of hand — the stock will be wide-ranging and may be particularly useful for providing background information on a topic. If you are tackling a new subject or failing to grasp an essential concept in your studies, then a 'layman's guide' from the lending library may be just what you need. **Fiction** of all sorts will be represented (some of it in foreign languages).
Reference Library	Specially good for encyclopaedias, dictionaries, directories and all the more expensive reference books. You cannot normally borrow from here but study tables and chairs are provided. This is the heart of the library where all the more difficult requests are dealt with. In here you will probably find all the more specialised periodicals (the lighter and more general interest ones in the lending area). Always ask if you cannot see the periodical you need.
Children's Library	For toddlers to teenagers. Story and information books similar to those in a school library. Often very good if you need pictures or illustrations. Staff can often be very helpful with study or homework problems. You may find that this part of the library includes a 'homework' room or area. This could be handy if you need somewhere quiet to work.
Newspapers and periodicals	A few libraries have a special room for these, but nowadays you are more likely to find them in the lending or reference libraries.
Commercial and business collections	Every large public library will have a special collection of trade and business information — sometimes housed as part of the reference library. This can be very useful if you are on a business studies course.

Library departments

Technical Library — Much will depend on what sort of town you live in whether you have one of these. If your city is very dependent on industry then the chances are that there will be a good technical library with specialised staff to help.

Art Collections — These are sometimes housed with the city's art gallery and will cover more than just pure art. Architecture, design and even fashion and costume may be part of these and most of them will have large collections of slides.

Government publications — These are very important sources of information and cover a huge area of everyday life. So much is published by **HMSO (Her Majesty's Stationery Office)** that many libraries have a separate department and staff just to deal with these. Statistics, trade, industry, education, food and farming etc as well as all Parliamentary proceedings provide students with a mass of material.

Special needs — This is not strictly a department but a service provided by many libraries. All libraries will make provision for people who may be **handicapped** in different ways. The most obvious thing you are likely to see is a shelf of **large-print** books but that is really only the tip of the iceberg. If you, or any of your friends, have trouble getting up the stairs into the library, or need special facilities of any sort, then do ask. Many libraries run special services (and have librarians whose sole job it is to organise this). You can often have books delivered to your door if you cannot get to the library. Some libraries also have special equipment, like **magnifiers**, either to use in the library or that you can borrow to use at home. For blind or partially sighted 'readers' there will also be lots of books on **cassettes**.

● *Tip* Public libraries are free to everyone. Find out what you have near you and use it to help you in your studies.

How To... Books
Opening Doors of Opportunity

A major series of self-help paperbacks packed with valuable information on new opportunities in today's fast-changing world. Each of these user-friendly handbooks gives clear up-to-date information and advice, prepared by experts, and complete with checklists for action and self-assessment material. The guides will save you time and money by supplying essential information which is often hard to find.

Helpfully clear layout with illustrations and cartoons, glossary, useful sources, index. Each 215 x 135mm, £4.95 approx.

You can't afford to miss the 'How To . . . series'

How to Get That Job Joan Fletcher
A guide for job hunters of all ages.
0 7463 0326 2

How to Pass Exams Without Anxiety David Acres
A step by step guide to removing stress and achieving success in exams at every level.
0 7463 0334 3

How to Live and Work in Australia Laura Veltman
The unique handbook for all those considering employment and residence 'Down Under'.
0 7463 0331 9

How to Live and Work in America Steve Mills
Packed with new ideas on home life, leisure, travel, social and business opportunities.
0 7463 0323 8

How to Help Your Child at School John West-Burnham
Vital information and advice for every concerned parent.
0 7463 0329 7

How to Enjoy Retirement Harry Gray
Utilising a lifetime's skills and experience for a happy and productive retirement.
0 7463 0323 8

How to Claim State Benefits Martin Rathfelder
Making sense of the system.
0 7463 0505 2

Dozens more titles in preparation. For details please contact Dept BPA.

Northcote House Publishers Ltd., Harper & Row House, Estover Road, Plymouth PL6 7PZ, United Kingdom.
Tel: Plymouth (0752) 705251 Telex: 45635.

2
Your Information Supermarket

You have made it to the library, and stand surrounded by perhaps thousands and thousands of books, little sign of any staff and no clue as to where you should ask or even what departments might exist. (This is the worst scenario you could find — it is most unlikely you will ever find such a bad library! If you do, complain loud and long to whoever is in charge. However, even in the best run and sign-posted libraries, it is not always easy to find the book, or even the subject area, you need. This chapter offers vital first-aid to make the job much easier. Remember, though, that using a library is a little like learning to drive a car. No-one expects an L-driver to master all the techniques in the first lesson; likewise, the more you use a library, the simpler it will become and also more rewarding and more fun. Let's assume you find yourself in a completely strange library.

GETTING YOUR BEARINGS

Look around and get some idea of the geography of the building. Are there separate departments such as Lending or Reference? Can you spot any notices telling you what is where? Is there an organised, tidy but welcoming entrance? Are the notices professional-looking and with plenty of current information? Take your time, and don't feel rushed.

Asking for help

If you have been lucky in your library, your second step may be to go straight to the department you need, having found all the directions and information in the entrance. However, this also presupposes you already know exactly what you want (and where to find it). This is unlikely unless you are clutching a prepared reading list and know that what you need is to be found in, say, the Technical Library.

● *Tip* If in doubt, find a librarian.

You are most likely to find staff on hand in the Lending Library and most libraries will place these on the ground floor and close to the entrance in a fairly obvious place. You may find a desk marked *Readers Adviser* or similar title; if so, make a bee-line for that since the librarian there will be specially trained to help borrowers, and know where to direct you. If there is no such desk, go to the library counter. If you want to borrow books you may be asked to fill in a simple form, but if yours is a college library, you may just be asked to show your union card.

THE CATALOGUE

Having been directed to the section or department you need, how do you find the specific book? If you are in a large library, there may be two or three shelves at least on your topic; finding the book you need may be like looking for a needle in a haystack. It's time now to get to grips with the **library catalogue** and **classification** system. Don't despair — both these tools are quite simple! Indeed, compared to many skills you will have already mastered, they are very easy. Some earlier librarians, it must be said, used to wrap the whole process up in mystery and mystique, but librarians today are keen for their 'customers' to understand and be able to use all the information tools they provide.

Noting down what you want

Before you start looking for the catalogue (or around the shelves), jot down a checklist of what you need. This will help you to define what you want and make it much easier to choose the right part of the catalogue.

CHECKLIST
1. Do I know the **author** of the book I want?
2. Do I know the **title** of the book I want?
3. Is there a particular **subject** I want, rather than a particular book?
4. What else is important? Do I need a **recent** publication? Do I need **maps**, **graphs**, **illustrations** or anything else like that?
5. Do I need a book at all — would a **video**, **cassette**, **slide**, or something else be more useful to me?

Using the catalogue

A catalogue is just a list of everything the library contains. If you are in a large library with lots of departments, check whether the catalogue lists everything or only the books in one department. If what you want is not there, it may be in the Reference or Commercial Libraries.

The catalogue

Catalogues come in all shapes and sizes, and more and more are computerised. However, many libraries still have the wooden drawer type with thousands of individual typed cards in them. It doesn't matter what the catalogue actually *looks* like — the basic arrangement will still be the same: you should be able to get the same answers whether your library is into high-tech or still back in the dark ages. There should be instructions on how to use the catalogue but if you are not sure, ask one of the library assistants for a demonstration — it is very easy to miss some of the useful information in a catalogue if you don't fully understand its arrangement.

Whatever sort of catalogue you find, it should be able to answer all these questions:

- Has the library a book by David Chrystal called *Linguistics*?
- Where is it shelved?
- What else has the library got by David Chrystal?
- I don't know who wrote it, but is there a book called *Manwatching*?
- Where will I find books on nuclear energy?
- I need an illustration of a stage-coach — what books are there on stage coaches in the library and do they have pictures?
- Has the library got the new edition of *Stanley Gibbons World Stamp Catalogue*?
- Does the catalogue entry refer to a book or some other form like a record or a video?

The library catalogue, whether it is on cards or on microfiche, will always have an **author index** and a **subject index**, both arranged alphabetically. Sometimes, these two files may be in one sequence but other libraries may keep them separate. Like everything else, there can be many different ways of arranging a catalogue, but if you can learn quickly how yours works, it will save you a lot of time in the future.

Microfiche

It is becoming more common nowadays to find a catalogue on strips of **microfiche**. You select the appropriate strip, place it in a desk-top reader which magnifies it, and you can then read the information normally. Microfiches take up much less space than the old card catalogues. If yours is a library with lots of different departments or branches, then it is easy for it to keep a full catalogue of everything it holds. This was impossible before as it was so expensive to make copies of all the thousands of catalogue cards.

- *Tip* Ask for a lesson on the catalogue and do yourself a good turn for the future!

UNDERSTANDING THE CLASSIFICATION SYSTEM

Learn how to make the **classification system** work for you. Some borrowers find it hard to believe that the odd numbers, letters or even symbols are there to help and not to hinder! Once you understand the basic idea behind the system your library uses then you'll find it all that much easier.

Libraries have had to work out ingenious ways of organising their books so that they, and their borrowers, can pick out one specific book. It's sometimes hard enough with your own books at home to find the one you want! You know exactly what you want, you know you have it somewhere, but somehow can't lay your hands on it. Imagine, then, the problems of a very large collection used by all sorts of different people, and you can begin to see why some sort of order is necessary.

Actually, we all **classify** all the time, sometimes without realising we are doing it — knives in one compartment, forks in the other. Supermarkets are past masters at the art — soap powders in that corner, baked beans on that shelf. The only difference with books (this is why it's a more complex system) is that it is not obvious from the outside 'packaging' what is inside. And, of course, there are so many more different items.

Books on insects, say, come in all shapes and sizes, different colours and may be hardback or paperback. Their appearance is no guide at all to their contents. Titles can be little help, too.

For these reasons, systems had to be devised which could overcome all these problems. There are now about three tried and tested schemes which a library can use to sort out its non-fiction stock. (Fiction will normally be in alphabetical order of author).

All about Dewey

The **Dewey Decimal Classification** system is the one you are most likely to meet and the chances are it's the one your own library will use. Melvil Dewey was an American who decided many years ago to divide all human knowledge into broad groups. Then, by the simple method of giving all of the subjects a number, he could relate subjects to each other. It sounds a great idea in theory, but we can soon realise some of the pitfalls. For example, new topics are constantly appearing: Dewey never even dreamed of space flight. Also, his idea of what went together is not necessarily everyone else's.

However, Melvil Dewey's scheme is still better than most and for this reason many libraries adopted it and still use it today. It is a basically simple idea to make a number stand for a subject name, and it does mean that anyone who can count can use the system easily. Dewey used every number from 000-999 and all the decimal places in between as well. The table shows his main groupings.

THE DEWEY CLASSIFICATION	
000-099	All the books which cover *all* knowledge. Encyclopaedias, for example, and books about librarianship.
100-199	Philosophy
200-299	All religions
300-399	Sociology and economics
400-499	Languages
500-599	Natural science
600-699	Applied science
700-799	Arts, crafts, sports
800-899	Literature (most libraries put in here books about authors and literary criticism — not the novels themselves — but you will find poetry and plays here).
900-999	History and geography

Each of these main sections from 0 to 9, Dewey divided up in more detail. For example Natural Science:

500 General Science
510 Mathematics
520 Astronomy
530 Physics
540 Chemistry

and so on.

This means that all books which start with the figures 54 will be about chemistry in some way or another. As a general rule, the longer the number, the more specialised will be the subject of the book. For instance, a book called *The Structural Effects on Equilibria in Organic Chemistry* would have the number 547.1392. With Dewey's classification system we can look for a specific number on the shelves. Even the most unusual or specialised topics will have a number.

Two other things to remember:

- It often happens that a book will cover two subject areas, e.g. *The Geology of Yorkshire*. Do you look for the Dewey number for geology or Yorkshire? The librarian has to decide where he/she thinks most people are likely to look for it and put it there — but that does not mean that some people will not look in the other place. The (subject) catalogue overcomes this particular problem, so remember always to check there.
- Since books come in all shapes and sizes, shelving them can be very difficult, and also very wasteful on space. For this reason, many libraries will have an **oversize** section where all the big books are kept separately, but in the same order. This should always be marked in the catalogue: remember to check there for your particular topic.

OTHER TIPS TO HELP YOU

1. **Periodical and magazine lists.**

All big libraries will have a list (usually in alphabetical order) of the title of all the periodicals they take. If it is a large library with lots of departments, then it should also tell you where to find them. Ask in the Lending or Reference libraries of a Public Library and at the main issue desk if you are using your college library. This list should also tell you how long the library has taken the magazine, and how far back they keep copies.

2. **Reading lists**

You may have been given a list by your teacher. This may be general background reading, or essential reading needed to complete your work. Either way, don't throw these lists away: they can save you hours of work in tracking down suitable books and may come in useful months after your original assignment.

Often a library in a school or college will compile their own reading lists on topics they know are important to the students (it saves librarians a lot of work if they have a basic list which can then be just updated as well as being useful for the student enquirers). There are also many published booklists on a huge variety of topics. Always ask about any lists that could help you.

3. **Library guides and instruction tours**

Many libraries issue guides to their services and their collections. Whether you are using your college library or a public library, always ask for one of these. It is free. At the very least it should tell you about opening hours, how to join, and what sort of special services your library offers. Many of these guides will include a plan or map of the library — very important if it houses a large collection.

Most libraries in education run **courses** on how to use the library. Sometimes these are just offered to new students, and are really only brief introductions. But often they continue over the whole session, becoming more specialised and directly geared to the information needs of particular courses. Do take advantage of anything like this on offer at your college.

4. **Tapes, records, videos, etc**

Does your library include these in its collection? If so, are they housed separately or perhaps listed in a different catalogue? A college library will probably have all the necessary 'hardware' to play these in the library. "A picture is worth a thousand words" — there could well be instances when this applies to you and your studies.

5. **Final tip**

Time and effort in getting to know your library and its staff will be time well spent. It will pay you dividends!

3
Using a Library for Study

Everyone has their own favourite place of study. Some find that only monastic quiet suits them, whilst others only seem able to work with Radio 1 as their constant companion. Only you can really decide which is the best place for you, but try to make sure that you are not just settling for the easy option where there is coffee on tap and your friend might phone up.

Be objective about your working environment and choose one that will help you achieve concentrated work. Most people, unless they are very lucky, have only one or two options but it can be critical to make the right choice.

WORKING AT HOME

Home is where most people do their work — it is usually warm, you have your own 'space' to work in and sometimes other people to ask if you get stuck. But blaring television, younger brothers or sisters quarrelling and family comings and goings are not conducive to any sort of work. You may kid yourself that distractions do not interrupt you but if you can still work with all that going on around you, then you must be a genius!

WORKING IN A LIBRARY

Your college, school or local public library are the other most obvious places for you to work, and for many students these will be the first choice. The school library may be restricted in its opening hours, which can be a problem, but college libraries are usually open for longer hours and may have more facilities. Either sort should provide study space and also the books and materials needed for your course. The staff are also usually trained and experienced in helping students. If neither of these are possibilities for you (you may live too far away to travel back in again) then try your local public library. It will probably have a much larger stock than your school or college and, if there is a large reference department, then it will almost certainly have study space. The chances are, too, that it will be open for much longer hours than either of the others.

> ● *Tip* Try to make working arrangements to suit *your* needs and avoid considerations that have nothing to do with the work you want to do.

HOW TO STUDY

Once you have settled on 'where' it is time to think of the 'how'. This means looking in detail at what you have to do, then deciding on the best possible approach. It's rather like driving a car — you use different techniques for motorway driving or busy urban traffic although the basic driving skills are common to both.

Learn efficient study techniques and, most importantly, learn how to apply them in differing situations so saving you time, effort and frustration. There are many short-cuts you can take: they not only make it easier to find and assimilate the information, but also make the task in hand so much more satisfying and rewarding.

Here are some of the more important 'short cuts'. Like everything else, as you get better at it, you will start to develop more sophisticated techniques of your own.

Reading short cuts

Whether you enjoy reading or not, the chances are that you will sometimes have to plough through tedious or dull material. This may be a textbook, background reading or supplementary material of one sort or another, all or some of which may not be to your taste. However, there are approved short cuts which help you to get the essentials without having to read the book from cover to cover.

Scanning

Firstly, **scanning**. Everyone does this at some time — flicking through the newspaper to find the TV programmes, picking up paperbacks in the bookshop and reading the odd sentences. These are really 'study techniques' that meet all sorts of eventualities. The best way to use them is when searching for specific information but having neither the time nor the need to read the whole book. Clues will be dotted around the book. Look for all these:

- **The Preface** or **Introduction** if the book has one. This will usually explain the purpose of the book and for whom it is intended. If you want an easy layman's guide to nuclear energy, there is little point in wasting time on a book that has been written for the professional scientist. This introduction will also often tell you about the **scope** of the book — what has been included and what has been left out.

- **Contents list.** This is a very useful study aid. By means of a quick scan you can tell very quickly if the book is relevant or not.

- **Chapter headings.** These have a similar 'guideline' effect as the contents list but they may sometimes be more detailed so giving you much more idea of the contents.

- **Paragraph headings.** Most writers use a new paragraph for each new idea or new development. By scanning the start of these you can often judge whether or not you need to read the whole section. Sometimes publishers help (as with this book) by using blacker or heavier type to emphasise important points, so check for that as well.

- **Index.** Most non-fiction books will have an index. Check for names or **keywords** of your topic. If the book lacks an index, then check all the other 'aids' so as not to waste valuable time. Most well-researched and authoritative books will have an index so you should perhaps beware of any that do not.

- **Names**, **titles** or other significant words. Scan the pages for these and ignore everything else. Make a list of words to look out for and just scan the pages for them.

Let's take a specific example. Your topic is Charlotte Brontë and you have discovered a very comprehensive (and very large) book on English literature in the library. You suspect that somewhere in all that maze will be the information you need. Try to break the problem down into smaller questions.

1. How is the book **arranged?** If it is alphabetical by names of authors, then you are home and dry. Is it historical or chronological? If so, do you know enough about Charlotte to make a guess at her approximate period?
2. What **clues** does the book have? Check for index, contents, chapter titles.
3. Section or paragraph **headings**? Capital letters or blacker type for quick reference?

Many books can be used just like a telephone directory. You need just one piece of information from the book: learn how to extract this quickly, and you will save hours of time and also give yourself the satisfaction of a new skill learned.

Skimming

Secondly **skimming**. All this means is that once you have found the right chapter or section of a book, your eyes will flick over the print looking for keywords, dates or names, to find out if what you really want is there. Let's take Charlotte Brontë again — you already know a fair bit about *Jane Eyre* but you have been asked also to include an examination of *Shirley* in your essay. You therefore skim across the page just looking for the word *Shirley* and not bothering to read anything else until you find that one important word. The whole aim of skim-reading is to **abstract** the important and key parts of the passage without having to read each and every word in the book.

Practise both these reading short cuts. You are probably already skilled in using them without realising it. They save hours of time and will pay dividends — not only in the time saved but also in the lack of frustration and boredom when you plough through a book for a small but vital snippet of information.

Note-taking

Why bother about taking notes? After all, you have textbooks, libraries, teachers or lecturers on hand to ask, so why go to all the bother?

There are three or four good reasons why note-taking is important for most students. Research projects which have studied this in detail have confirmed that students who take good notes do consistently better than those who take none, or do so but in a careless and slipshod fashion.

Reasons for taking good notes include the following:

- From your notes you have a **permanent and personal record** of the lecture or of the information extracted from a book.

- However concentrated your listening may be in a lecture, it is impossible totally to **recall** all that has been said. In the same way remembering what you have read in a book presents the same difficulties.

- The act of taking notes is a good discipline, and keeps you on top of your subject.

- Good note-taking is **active learning**.

Good lecturers will always try, by their very delivery, to make it easy for you to pick out the important points in their lecture so that you can come out with good clear notes. What you are really doing is the tradi-

Note-taking

tional English **précis**, but from speech not a printed text. Names, dates, happenings are all clues to listen for and write down; if you have these you can always go back and fill in the gaps afterwards. Surprisingly enough, most students find they can keep up with a lecture and even if their notes are a sentence or so behind the speaker they still do not get lost.

Some people take notes more easily by making a kind of spiders web of connecting ideas, developments, names etc. Note-taking does not necessarily mean always writing in lines on an exercise book so, if you like, experiment to find the best method for you. Again, the method may vary depending on the topic.

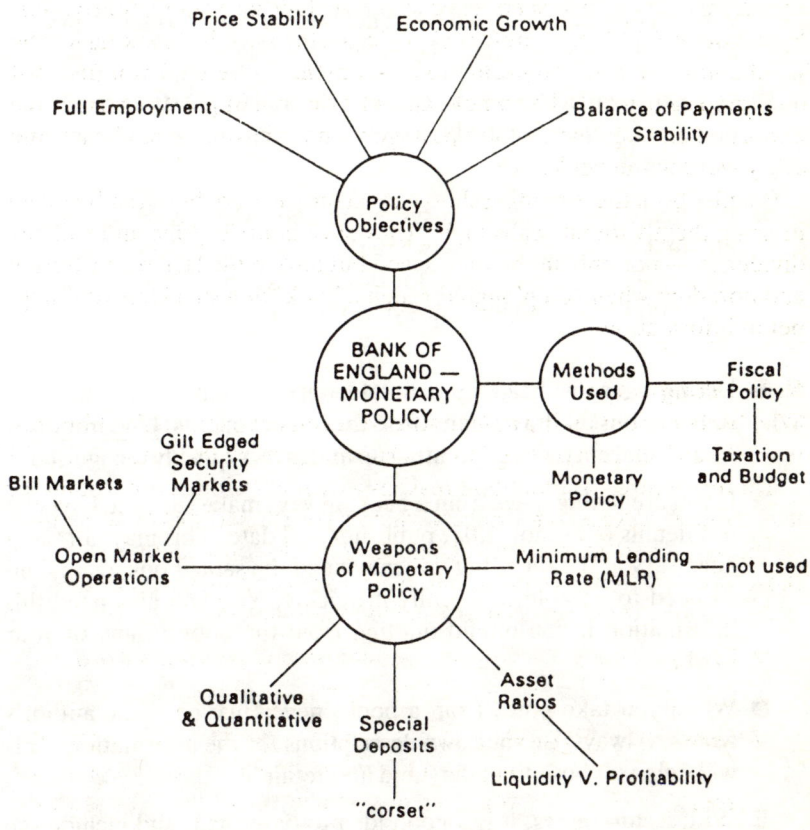

Sample pattern note — The Bank of England and Monetary Policy

Note-taking tips; you can do any or all of these and they can all help in various ways.

- Use different **coloured** pens and pencils to highlight particular aspects.

- Leave wide **margins** so that you can alter or add to the information.

- **Write up** your notes 'tidily' as soon as possible after the lecture. This is one of the best study techniques in its own right. It makes you aware of any gaps or misunderstandings in your notes so that you can rectify these whilst it is still fresh in your memory. Also, you will find that the act of re-writing helps to fix the information in your mind and provides a kind of painless revision.

- Use **loose-leaf** notebooks so that you can add to or extract from your notes easily and effectively. You can also re-sort the information at any time if you need to.

- If it helps you, work out a system of **abbreviations** or 'shorthand' but make sure you know what they all mean! Don't chop and change — a cardinal recipe for disaster. Keep a list at the back of your notebook of all the abbreviations you have used, to avoid confusion.

- Use **paragraphs**, **headings**, **capital letters** — whatever you like and suits you best to draw attention to the important bits. <u>Underlining</u> is a quick and easy way of pointing up and is very quickly recognised.

- If you are **taking notes from a book**, always make sure you have the full details of author, title, publisher and date. This may not seem necessary at the time, but you may need the same book again, and so need to be able to identify it quickly. You will also need this information if you intend quoting from the book in any of your work.

- When you take notes from a book, never just copy the author's words. Always **use your own descriptions** for the information. This will help you both to understand and retain it.

- With **lecture notes**, it is a good idea to date them and include the name of the lecturer. This may not seem vital at the time, but if your course is a long one with many different teachers, it may be important at exam time to know who taught what particular part of the course and who can help with any problems.

- Good notes are one of the main recipes for success — **don't skimp them**. What else can help?

Memory training techniques

Remember that old party game where someone brings in a tray of different objects? You have to look at them for a short time, then the tray is taken away, and you have to remember them all. It's a good memory-training game, as are many card games. Anything that helps you to recall facts is useful; people will often devise their own **word associations** to help them retain facts.

As long as it is clearly retained in your mind, it doesn't matter how weird it seems to your friends. **Repetition**, **word association**, **writing up notes** are all good ways to improve your memory. Just as an athlete trains his body, so you can train your brain to work more efficiently. You may find that it helps to talk over your studies. Indeed, some people find it pays to actually teach someone else, since it often helps to clarify their own knowledge.

Planning

As the old adage says, 'A well planned job is a job half done'. This is one of the keys to any successful operation. If you plan things badly you will not only waste a lot of time, you will end up with a piece of work that neither represents what you were asked to do nor what you could have produced if you had gone about it differently.

Often you will have a **project**, **assignment** or **essay** to do. Before you start, spend a few minutes thinking about how to tackle it. For example:

- Make yourself a cup of tea or coffee and get relaxed.
- Take a sheet of paper and make some rough notes.
- Read the question through carefully, and start thinking of some of the things you will have to do.
- Try to use the step-by-step guide set out below.

Everything you need to finish a successful piece of work can be broken down into easy steps. The simplest thing is to plan your approach by writing down a list of **headings**. This works for any sort of study, and will help you collect and use your information quickly.

It will also help you get more out of your library. *You* won't be one of those panicky students rushing about from shelf to shelf, pulling books off at random, and finding nothing of any use. Yours will be a *structured* and *planned* approach, and you'll have the satisfaction of achieving what you want quickly and easily. You could start like this:

PROJECT CHECKLIST	ROUGH NOTES
1. What **information do I need?**	....
2. **Where** can I get it?	....
3. **How** do I find it?	....
4. How can I **use** it?	....
5. What **notes** will I make?	....
6. Have I got **all** I need?	....
7. How am I going to **present** the information?	....
8. Have I done **everything** needed?	....

Let's take each of these in turn, and see what they involve. What do you already know about the subject? You might have a few ideas and facts in your head, or in notes. Or perhaps you have to start from scratch. The sort of information you need might include some facts, statistics, names or short summaries of information. You might need to see some photographs, drawings, diagrams or maps, to make up your own sketch illustrations.

- What **guidelines** has your teacher given you? For example you might need to gather information from people outside school, or to use a questionnaire. Or perhaps you have got to examine certain statements and get evidence to back them up or challenge them.
- How **detailed** has the project to be? Would a couple of sheets do, or are you expected to work up a big folder? Think about how many pages you will prepare, and how many documents or illustrations.
- How much **extra information** do you need? Are some facts and figures going to be hard to get? Which ones?
- How **long** is the finished project to be? Not too long and not too short: enough to make it reasonably complete and interesting.

If you are not sure about some of these points, have a word with your teacher.

Time-tabling

This is a very important part of the whole planning process. It is not always easy, at the start of a project, to know how long each part will take but one useful idea is to start, as it were, at the end. Ask yourself:

1. How **long** do I want the project to be?
2. How **much** do I know already?
3. How much **new** information must I find?
4. Will this new information be **difficult** to understand or will it build on what I already know?
5. What are the chances of **finding** this additional information quickly? (This means you need to know what library facilities exist and how far they can help you.)
6. How **long have I got** before the work has to be handed in?
7. Based on previous experience, how **easy** do I find it to write up the project or essay once I have found all the material?

If it is a subject you are familiar with, or if you have been asked to present the work in a more detailed way than before, then you may have problems deciding your priorities.

It's a little like looking for a particular street in London from a road map of the British Isles — you have few clues or prior knowledge to fill in the gaps. If you are really stuck, go back and ask your teacher, but making

A library makes an ideal place for study.

Time-tabling

a time and study plan will go a long way towards sorting out some of these problems. A sample timetable could run like this:
1. Check with teacher over proposed length.
2. Go over lecture notes for relevant information.
3. Make a list of gaps in information.
4. Discover sources to fill these.
5. Accumulate all necessary information and consider how best to present it.
6. Do rough draft of project.
7. Consider this critically and objectively.
8. Re-write, bearing in mind what was actually asked for.
9. Hand in, with some satisfaction of work having been well planned and well done.

I made a plan for writing this book which went something like this:

(a)	Do contents and chapter heading lists	Time, 2 days
(b)	Write first draft	40 days
(c)	Second draft	37 days
(d)	Third and final draft	21 days
(e)	Final checking	14 days

I worked this out on the basis of writing about 1,000 words per day. I also included all the time for reading and information-seeking as well as spare days when for one reason or another I did not get my work done, like three weeks' holiday in the middle!

This planning gave me three very important 'spin-offs';

- It helped me to sort out what needed doing, and in what order.
- It made me consider the time factor and how to fit the work into a finite period.
- It gave me a framework in which to operate and clear daily discipline.

The timetable itself becomes a great motivator and reinforcer. It can help you stick at it when you might otherwise be tempted to laze around. The planning of both the work, and the time schedule, are vital for a good project.

Subject and skills

Most subjects have particular skills that are relevant to them. If you are studying such a subject then time spent learning these techniques will pay off in the future. Many of these will be part of your normal lectures — for instance all geographers will quickly learn how to interpret maps; scientists will become familiar with the way experiments are written up, and all the signs and symbols used.

As with all these study skills, the trick is to know which technique to use to help in the specific task. If you find yourself having to use unfamiliar tools, or extract information from an unfamiliar graphic source, then never be afraid to ask. Librarians will always be happy to help, your subject teacher will be an obvious source and if all these fail, then ask a fellow student studying that subject.

> ● *Tip* Everything in this chapter is designed to help you make more effective use of **your time** and **your brain**. Don't waste either!

The Gabbitas-Thring Guide to Independent Further Education

Gabbitas-Thring, the world renowned educational advisory trust, with over 100 years' experience in the field of education, provides parents, teachers, careers advisers and students with the first really comprehensive source book on the growing independent sector in British Education today. With more than 600 detailed entries and informative articles by leading specialist contributors, this new *Guide* meets a real need for objective consumer information on private Schools, Colleges and Training Establishments in all areas of Further Education from GCE and secretarial to technical and domestic arts and, as such, will provide an invaluable new reference source for everyone concerned with the highest standards in Further Education.

1986-87 Edition, £9.95 paperback. *Available Now.* 0 7463 0388 2.

Northcote House Publishers Ltd., Harper & Row House, Estover Road, Plymouth PL6 7PZ, United Kingdom. Tel: Plymouth (0752) 705251 Telex: 45635.

4
Using Books for Reference

Both libraries and books come in all sorts of shapes and sizes, from the massive storehouse of a large university library or the 24 volume encyclopaedia, to the pocket-sized paperback or the small mobile library. One of the tricks of effective library use is to be able to find your way through the labyrinth and pick off the shelves what you want quickly and easily.

It is not always that simple, though, as books like cars come in different models. The 'sports car type book' is usually fairly small but provides fast answers to basic questions. The family estate car is more cumbersome but holds much more; books like that can help with more detailed and considered information. The trick is to know what is available, and then to choose the right ones for you.

REFERENCE BOOKS

The term **reference** book can mean any book that you use to find out information (as opposed to the latest thriller read purely for pleasure). However, most people use the term to mean the bigger and more weighty tomes found in large libraries. These are the books most often used by the serious student, and rarely available for loan. Many of these books are published in standard **formats** and arrangements, and if you can get to know these and be confident in choosing the appropriate one, you will save a lot of time.

Encyclopaedias and **dictionaries** are probably the two best known sorts of reference books and very few people will not have used these at one time or another. However, be warned; publishers are apt to use these two words quite indiscriminately, so never go just by what a book *calls* itself but only by what is *inside* it. The real difference between an encyclopaedia and a dictionary is in the amount of information each contains. Dictionaries are usually shorter with perhaps only one or two lines of explanation (and usually in only one volume). Encyclopaedias, though, can have whole articles that stretch sometimes for pages and in themselves can provide a complete introduction to a subject. A classic example of an encyclopaedia that calls itself a dictionary is *Groves Dictionary of Music and Musicians* — a large multi-volume work packed with very detailed information.

> ● *Tip* Take no notice of what a book is called — go by what is inside.

Encyclopaedias

Encyclopaedias come in two distinct types:

- The sort that covers **all knowledge**, usually arranged alphabetically by subject, and giving perhaps a short paragraph on each topic or, like *Encyclopaedia Britannica*, very long scholarly articles. This type is very useful if you want an introduction to a subject about which you know very little.

- **Subject encyclopaedias** which take just one area and give detailed (and often fairly specialised) information. Van Nostrand's *Science Encyclopaedia* is an example of this. If you already know a little about a topic, this type can be very useful to extend your knowledge, or help in defining a tricky point.

How to use encyclopaedias

Points to remember when consulting encyclopaedias are:

1. Entries are nearly always **alphabetical by subject**, but sometimes you need to look under one or two headings. For example if you want Anglo-Saxon literature you may need to look both under that heading and also under the names of individual writers such as Bede.

2. All the major encyclopaedias have **indexes**. Indeed, *Encyclopaedia Britannica* has a whole volume devoted to this. Indexes are there to cope with the very problems instanced in 1, and to try to lead you on to related material scattered elsewhere in the other volumes. Never underestimate the value of a good index (usually prepared by professional indexers); it is the equivalent of a good browse round the shelves.

3. Check the **date of publication**, particularly if you need reliable technical or scientific information. However, if what you need is Latin grammar or music theory then the date will be less important since the information won't have altered much.

Encyclopaedias and dictionaries

4. Encyclopaedias are essentially **starter packs** where you will find the basic answer to your question, but not always the more specialised or lengthy answer. For this you will need to use other sources.

5. As a general rule, it is true to say that if you know nothing about a subject, then one of the all-encompassing encyclopaedias will at least start you off on the quest. If you already know a little, then one of the subject ones may help you to know much more and build on your existing knowledge.

6. It's always a good idea, and can become a fascinating exercise, to look in **more than one publication** to see how entries differ and how much more, or less, information may be in one or the other. You may find that one publication has what you need just at the right level whereas another may be far too specialised (or too brief).

7. The best sort of encyclopaedias are really **authoritative** — in other words the articles in them are written by subject specialists and signed by them. Many of the articles in *Encyclopaedia Britannica* are very lengthy indeed, signed by the author, and include follow up reading lists; these become subject guides in themselves. But some of the cheaper and less scholarly encyclopaedias will have much sketchier information, and offer little more than dictionaries.

8. Encyclopaedias are virtually always in the **reference department** of the library. Rarely, if ever, are they allowed out on loan. They are there to satisfy requests for specific information which can be remembered or noted down quickly. Most of the general encyclopaedias will be shelved together, but the ones dealing with individual topics will probably be with the other books on that subject. Your knowledge of the layout of the library, as well as your skill with the catalogue and classification, will come in handy to locate what you need.

Dictionaries

Dictionaries are a very close relation to encyclopaedias and, as already has been said, it is sometimes impossible to distinguish the two. They also come in different guises but the one most people will be familiar with is the sort that tells you how to spell a word, or which tells you what an unfamiliar word means.

The range of Oxford dictionaries from the small *Concise* up to the large multi-volume *Oxford English Dictionary* are some of the best known of this type; all the foreign language dictionaries serve the same functions.

There are other types of dictionary, though, and some of the most helpful for students are the subject dictionaries which can help to unravel some of the problems when you are faced with 'jargon' words that you do not understand. Virtually all subjects have their own dictionary. It is worth finding the best one for your subject and becoming familiar with using it.

Many of the tips for using encyclopaedias work just as well for dictionaries; the cardinal point to bear in mind is *what* you need to find out.

- Is it just a meaning or a spelling? How much do you know already?
- Can you cope with technical or specialised language?
- Are you looking for a start into more detailed research?
- Are you just trying to find the answer to a quiz question?

Before you start, try to define the area and the extent of your search. That, in turn, will help you make the correct choice of sources.

One point to bear in mind is that all encyclopaedias, and to some extent dictionaries too, are very expensive. They cost a lot of the library's book money to keep up-to-date. Because of this, only the biggest public reference libraries or big colleges and universities can afford to hold a wide range of them. Small schools, branch libraries or even colleges just cannot afford to buy all the necessary reference works and keep them up-to-date. Check your nearest source and remember to check the **date** of publication if this is important to your subject.

What else should you know about? Apart from the two obvious ones just discussed there are a whole lot more useful types of books which can save much time and effort.

Directories

The obvious one here that everyone knows is the **telephone directory** (and do not underestimate the value of the yellow pages either — very handy for tracking down firms and manufacturers). Most professional associations, societies, industrial groups all issue — usually annually — lists of their members, but some of the most valuable directories for students are the **commercial directories** which exist for nearly every trade and profession, and are regularly updated. These could come in very handy for you if you need to write to firms in a particular industry, or to know who makes what. The best place to find a wide range of these is in the nearest Commercial Library (probably housed in the central public library), but you may find that large local firms will have all the directories that deal with their products and they may let you use them.

Yearbooks

A very similar animal to the directories but often including a wealth of current information updated annually and packed into a relatively small space. The most famous here is probably *Whitaker's Almanac*. This has a fantastic amount in it from a list of all MP's to the Roman calendar, postal regulations and annual expenditure on roads. If you have never seen this wonderful book, do spend some time dipping into it — it should be your first port of call if you need current information.

Handbooks

If you are a builder, a scientist, or in any of the other fields which include a lot of data, formulae or similar basic information then the chances are that somewhere there is a handbook to cover your subject. If you think of these as 'recipe' or 'how to do it' books then you will have a good idea of their contents. *Spons Workshop Receipts, Kempe's Engineers Handbook* and *The British Pharmacopoeia* are examples. Some of them may be aimed at the general reader but most are produced to meet a demand from professionals in the field. If you need this type of book, it really pays to check the publication date. This can be particularly critical in scientific topics, and in the social or welfare services where legislation may dramtically affect them.

Atlases, gazeteers

Really this is self-explanatory and most people will have used atlases many times. But remember they can come in all varieties from the old school 'capes and bays' which just show physical features to more sophisticated ones which perhaps deal solely with one topic like the spread of disease or the economy of a country. As with dictionaries and encyclopaedias you can find atlases to meet all sorts of queries — remember the historical ones if you are a history student. These are very handy to show changes of political power and boundaries.

Gazeteers are really part of the same genre and are often included in the same publication. Their main aim is to help you to locate precisely a certain **place**. They can be specially useful when a number of places have the same name. You might be surprised to discover how many San Franciscos there are in the world.

OTHER REFERENCE BOOKS

What else? Well, the list is really endless and although the ones mentioned earlier in this chapter will start you off, there are lots more that could help you. One of the problems for the student without access to a good library is that few reference books are found in bookshops, so it is impossible for people to know what exists. It's rather like trying to choose a meal in a restaurant when you cannot see the menu. If you find yourself

Other reference books

in this quandary, try to spend some time in your nearest large library. Ask your teachers, ask the librarians, and pick up all the clues you can from your reading. Often other books will be mentioned, a further reading list may be included and all these can lead you on into other areas which you might not have discovered for yourself. Keep notes of what you find as you go along. Just to give you some idea of what else you could expect to find, here are a few examples.

- *Keesings Contemporary Archives.* A most useful publication for anyone needing current international information. It comes out weekly, produces frequent indexes and details all that is going on in the world, politically and economically.

- *Oxford Companion To* . . . almost everything in the arts and literature fields is covered by this series. They are really like specialist encyclopaedias and are packed with useful information.

- *Books of Quotations.* Probably very familiar to you, but remember that many deal with different areas, may be arranged by subject, and can be used in all sorts of ways.

- *Who's Who* and other biographical dictionaries. If you want to find out about anyone, living or dead, then these could be your answer. The enormous multi-volume *Dictionary of National Biography* is the main standard source for Britain, but this is a very large work, and very expensive, so only large libraries will have it. However there are lots of one-volume works which most libraries do have and all you need to check is whether it only includes people who are still alive (as does *Who's Who*).

- One-off reference books. Some books cannot be fitted into any ready-made category but can be just what you need for an out of the way query. Look at *Brewers Dictionary of Phrase and Fable* to see what I mean. There is everything in here from the possible derivation of the term 'Old Nick' to where the term 'nick' comes from. If you are a crossword addict, this book is a must!

The one rule always to remember is that no-one, however specialised, can possibly remember all the sources of information in their field. Librarians are there to fill that gap. A librarian's role is *not* to be a subject specialist as such, but a specialist in *sources* of information.

- *Tip* Ask the information specialist.

5
Using a Library for Research

'Horses for courses' is an old saying, and one which still holds good when it comes to finding out what information you want and how to find it. The last chapter looked at some of the different sorts of reference books but there are lots of other equally important sources. For some subjects these are vital for a successful outcome to your search. As important as knowing about them is the ability to handle them with confidence.

- **First principle.** If the question is simple, then the chances are that finding the answer will be simple too.

For example, 'Who is the President of France?' This is quickly answered from *The Statesman's Year Book, Whitaker's Almanac* or some other year book. Possible pitfall — make sure you look at the date of publication and that you have the current edition. If you suspect that the name may have changed recently, then check in *Keesings*. Remember, too, that only large libraries will have a selection of up-to-date year books but a simple query like this should not really cause any problem. *Tip* — never make things more complicated than they need to be.

- **Second principle.** Even if the question looks complicated, it can still be broken down into a series of steps.

For example, 'Consider the effects of falling oil prices on the economy of Scotland.' There is no single reference or text book which is going to give you the whole answer to this. You will have to collect information from a number of sources before you can begin to put it together as a finished project.

The main elements that you will probably have to consider will be both **economic** and **sociological** and possibly the **political** implications will also need investigating. You have to start this project from the existing situation; without knowing what effect the oil boom has had up to now, there is no way you can predict what might happen in the future. Your first thrust, then, is to discover as much as possible about the present. After that you can begin to think about what may happen later. The chances are that you already have some background knowledge to help you in perhaps economics or sociology and you should always use that as a starting point. Let's now break down the question into smaller pieces:

1. Statistical information — **how much** revenue comes in at the moment to Scotland from oil?
2. Is it **concentrated** in certain areas or does it spread across the country?
3. Is most of it **British** money or does some of it go straight abroad?
4. How has the oil money affected the **infrastructure**, i.e. schools, houses, food prices?
5. Has the **leisure industry** expanded as a direct result?
6. What about **subsidiary industries**? Will they be affected?

The answers to these should give you the basis of the present situation and some idea as to where your project might be leading. Now for the second phase.

1. What alternative **employment** might there be if oil fails?
2. Is there **anything else** that might take the economic place of oil in Scotland?
3. Are there **examples from other places** with which you could draw parallels?

Clearly, a good answer is not something you can dash off in half an hour, but even the most complicated question can be broken down into small steps. It's also important to remember that this breaking down can often give you the **structure** for your finished answer. Look at the Scottish example — with a few minor changes and modifications you have got the plan for your essay. You can never be too inflexible over this, though. You may turn up interesting information which could dramatically alter the emphasis of your argument.

● *Tip* Time spent defining your problem is never wasted.

You might say that this separation into small segments of your topic leaves you with more problems than you had before; instead of one question to answer you now have lots more and little idea where to find the answers to any of these. But really it's not as difficult or as complicated as it may first appear!

A research checklist

Making a plan
1. First, go through your **existing material** — any relevant lecture notes, textbooks or readings that you already have.
2. Make a note of any **other books** or **periodicals** that are mentioned in them.
3. **Jot down** what information you have already found or already know.
4. On the basis of your original question 'breakdown', make a list of all the **information gaps** you need to fill.
5. Consider what you know about **sources** of information for this particular project — will most of it come from books? How up-to-date must it be? Will that mean periodicals rather than books? What about newspaper articles?
6. Consider your own **library facilities**. Will your college or school be able to supply what you need? If not, do you know where else to go?

"Can you tell me to what extent oil has affected your infrastructure?"

Having decided on which library to use, you then have to try to find the answers to your questions. This is where some of the special techniques really come into their own; the preliminary effort you have put into getting to know your library will really pay off.

Always start from what you know and build on that. Next steps:

(a) Check the **library catalogue** for any books you know exist or any you have seen mentioned in reading lists. Remember to make a note of their classifications to save time later.

(b) Check the library **subject index** — first having made a list of all the important 'key' words in your topic. Note those classification numbers, too. Titles of books do not always reflect their contents very accurately. Spend time browsing around your subject area shelves.

(c) Having accumulated as much information as you can from the catalogue, start to **track down** all the items. Some of them will be no use at all (don't be too disappointed as this always happens and sometimes the most unlikely reference turns out to be just what you need). Remember to use the skimming and scanning techniques mentioned earlier and do not waste time trying to read a book all the way through.

(d) After you have seen as many of the books as you possibly can, **review the situation**. Go back to points 3 and 4 in your plan — what do you know now and what other gaps still exist? It may well be that, for this particular question, the gaps are in the current situation and the books you have found do not cover the latest picture of the drop in world oil prices for Scotland in particular.

Periodicals

This is where the whole field of **periodical literature** comes into its own. Many of us, when we think of magazines, tend to visualise the railway bookstall or the local newsagents. Unless you are a serious student, a librarian or a researcher you may have little idea of the huge number of specialised periodicals published worldwide every week. These are the backbone of much scientific and medical research in particular, but the value of all periodical literature to any research cannot be overlooked. Periodicals are important for five main reasons.

- **A book** takes anything up to two years to reach the bookshops from the time it is first thought of by either the author or the publisher. It is usually a fairly major undertaking for both parties and demands a lot of time and financial commitment. Books which deal with new advances in any subject can be out-of-date before they are published.

- **New knowledge** is advancing very rapidly and people working in all fields need to know quickly what is happening.
- **Short informative news** can be given speedily in periodicals from details of new research to reports of conferences and notices of meetings — all impossible in book form.
- Periodicals are relatively **inexpensive** to publish and mean that individuals can keep up-to-date in their own subject fairly easily.
- The major periodicals in all fields have a **worldwide circulation**. If you check the periodicals in any university library, you will find examples from all over the world and in all languages. Often specialised agencies exist to translate periodicals when the information they contain is considered too important to miss. Research workers worldwide can be united by these periodicals and share their problems or discoveries as well as keep abreast of the subject.

All this means that if you need current information you are going to have to refer to periodicals but, as with books, there are short cuts and easy ways of going about it. There is no way you have to plough through great piles of magazines in the hope that you will find the one specific article you need to finish off your project.

Let's look again at Scotland and the oil industry — there will probably be two sorts of information you need either from periodicals or newspapers.

- The more **specialised** publication with articles perhaps by economists for economists.
- More **general** articles found in newspapers like *The Times* or *The Guardian* which demand a reasonable knowledge but which are aimed at the interested layman rather than the professional.

Your problem is to find out *what* there is and *where* to find it.

"He knows it's my copy of Monthly Petroleum Abstracts."

Abstracts and indexes

Luckily this has been largely solved by a whole series of publications called **Abstracts** and **Indexes**. **Abstracts** are exactly what they say they are. In other words you get a short description of the original article together with full details of who wrote it, when, and in what publication. These *précis* are very useful as you can usually tell from them if it is worth your while looking for the original article or not.

Indexes are again just what they say. They just give you the author, title, original publication and date. But with these you get no description so it is not nearly so easy to decide how useful the article might be.

Abstracts and indexes cover all subject areas. Just as there are specialist dictionaries and encyclopaedias for each topic so these tools will also exist. They are all aimed at saving your time. Since they always have a subject index, it makes no difference if you have no idea of author or title. (For most periodical searches looking for the **subject** is by far the commonest approach).

> ● *Tip* There is often more than one abstract or index for each subject. Try to familiarise yourself with the ones you may need. Ask the librarian to help you.

Abstracts and indexes often come out once a month but there is usually a time-lag of around three months (sometimes longer) before an article in a periodical will be listed in the abstracting journal. This is because someone has to check all the articles in a periodical, list them, and possibly write the abstract. The editor of the publication then has to put all this information together, compile a complete subject and author list, get the whole thing printed and then distribute it.

> ● *Tip* You may have to check the last few editions of the major periodicals in your field as they will be too recent to have been abstracted.

Specialist abstracts and indexes are too expensive for small libraries to keep, so you will probably have to use your nearest university, poly or large reference library. All these tools, though, are of prime importance to researchers, so if you have any research going on near to you, you could approach that establishment to see if you could use theirs.

For both the project in hand and for future use, it is well worth finding out and noting the following:

- ● Which periodicals are important in my field?
- ● Which libraries stock them?
- ● Which abstracts and indexes cover these and where can I see them?
- ● Am I familiar with all these tools?

Project checklists

Back to Scotland and the project — let's recap on what you have already done:

— Broken the question down into component parts.
— Checked your own knowledge.
— Made a list of additional readings etc, that you found in 1.
— Made a list of known gaps.
— Chosen which library to use for further study.
— Checked the catalogue for relevant information and followed up all leads.
— Reviewed the situation with special reference both to gaps and the need for current information.
— Discovered the periodicals most suitable for your use and made a note of them.
— Become familiar with the abstracts and indexes for these periodicals.
— Checked the most recent copies of your selected periodicals.

The next and almost final step in the search for information is to review in detail what you have found, bearing in mind what you have been asked to produce. If you honestly feel you have done it all, then you can get down to the writing-up and presentation. If not then you may have to consider the following steps:

- Who else can I approach?
- Do I need more help from my teacher, or do I need to ask the librarian for more help over sources?
- Is the library I am using not good enough for my purpose?
- What possible alternatives might there be?

If you are reasonably happy about what you have done, here is a final checklist:
1. Have I covered *all* the points?
2. Have I found *new information* that I had not previously considered?
3. If so, does this alter the *overall plan*?
4. Should the *emphasis* be changed in any way?

All this chapter, so far, has been about what is technically called a **literature search**. All it really means is going in careful steps from what you already know to what you do not know, and building up the picture piece-by-piece.

- *Tip* Always start from what you know and go carefully and logically from that.

What else might you find useful?

Research facilities in a modern library.

Bibliographies
These come in all shapes and sizes. Basically they are just lists of books or periodical articles, usually dealing with just one topic. Sometimes they may be a list of all the books published in a particular year. The ones that will help you most are those that deal with a particular topic and bring together all the relevant published material about it. Sometimes you will find a list like this at the back of a textbook or at the end of an article. Major encyclopaedias also often include bibliographies at the end of the longer sections.

Whatever its size and wherever you find it, a bibliography is always a useful tool, pointing you in directions you might not have considered and suggesting new areas for investigation. Most libraries will have some of the larger bibliographies but only the bigger ones will have a comprehensive selection.

Reading lists
These are really bibliographies under another name, but often shorter and less comprehensive. You may be given one of these by your lecturer, listing books felt to be specially relevant. These are particularly useful as they often show which aspects of the topic the teacher feels are most important. Hang on to any of these you are given — they can come in very handy at revision time or for related work.

The Do-It-Yourself bibliography
It is a good idea to keep your *own* file of books or articles you have found useful. This helps not only your present work but exam revision, too. You will need this information if you want to quote from any books or articles in your work. If you have made your list correctly you will have no problem in identifying the same work any time in the future. You won't be one of those students looking for 'was it a large red book on the second to the bottom shelf?' Make sure you have all this down for each book:

Author	*Title*	*Publisher*	*Date*
Davies, H.	Wordsworth	Hamlyn	1980

It's also a good idea to note which library you found the book in, and its classification number there. Articles in periodicals need a slightly different treatment:

Author	*Title*	*Periodical*	*Vol. No.*	*Date*	*Pages*
Beswick, N.	Information systems and education	Education Library Bulletin	25 (2)	Summer 1982	1-14

This may seem finicky but it could save you much hassle in the future. If you ever wanted a photocopy of an article you would need all this information before you could order it from a library. If you really needed it years later there would be nothing more frustrating than being unable to track something down that you *know* exists.

If you can get hold of some cards the same size as libraries use for their catalogues this is the easiest way of keeping your bibliography. (Most office supply firms sell these cards, including index cards.) If you use these, you can add to or extract from the list as often as you like, change the order to suit particular purposes and generally be much more flexible than a bibliography kept in an old exercise book.

● *Tip* It's only a minute's job to keep a record of your sources of information — don't neglect it!

Working Abroad?
Harry Brown

● **The best-selling expatriate handbook, now in its 5th edition**

● **Authored by Britain's foremost specialist on expatriate affairs**

● **Completely revised and rewritten for 1986/87**

● **Practical, readable and completely authoritative**

● **Vital reading for 200,000 Britons going to work abroad each year**

● **Huge overall readership of 2 million working expatriates**

160 pp, 210 x 149 mm, £6.95 paperback. 0 7463 0383 1.

Northcote House Publishers Ltd
Harper & Row House
Estover Road, Plymouth PL6 7PZ
United Kingdom
Tel: Plymouth (0752) 705251
Telex: 45635

"As essential to the working British expatriate as his passport." — *Accountant Magazine.*

6
Related Sources

Your first call will be to libraries in your search for information, but there are lots of other places which can provide you with helpful advice and hard information. Some of these should be available locally; and if you live in a big town, probably all of them will be within a reasonable distance.

MUSEUMS

Don't think of museums as dusty old tombs full of glass cases of arrowheads or bits of broken pottery. If you haven't been into a museum lately you may be in for a shock! Most of them today are lively, well-designed places. They not only show off their collections in the best possible way, they interpret and help to make the past more understandable for all their visitors. Obviously, history in its broadest sense is the main province of all museums but it would be wrong to see them as only of interest to someone studying history or archaeology. After all, think of the **Science Museum** in London, full of working models, or the **Natural History Museum** with its marvellous insight into all forms of life. Museums come in all shapes and sizes and, like libraries, deal with all sorts of subjects.

Increasingly, local museums are springing up which concentrate on the industries of the area and give an insight into what life was like for the ordinary people working in the mills, steel works, or countryside. Many of these are housed in buildings which were themsleves old factories, so even the museum building has some historical interest. Staff in museums are very knowledgeable about their collections and very enthusiastic too, they will probably have access to all the specialised sources in their topic. These are some of the different museums you will find:

Your local town museum
This may have everything in it from bits of old pot to stuffed tigers. Much of what is in a local museum has probably been given by local worthies so

sometimes it seems a rag-bag of objects. This can have the effect of making them fascinating places as you never know what may be round the next showcase. What you will probably find in them all is anything to do with the history of the town and the area, but you will have to browse around to discover what else is there.

Industrial museums
These are springing up all over the place and can give a real feel for what the industry and lifestyle of a place was years ago. For a long time it was thought that only things that were very old or very valuable were worth putting in museums, but now it is realised that the life and work of ordinary people is in many ways more revealing. Increasing emphasis is placed on this aspect.

Industrial museums often have not only working models but the real old machinery repaired and in working order. If you are on a technical course of any sort, a visit to somewhere like this could be really worthwhile. Modern machines have often developed from very simple beginnings and these museums can show the various progressions as well as let you see exactly what they did. Historians will find these places marvellous sources — but so can everyone studying sociology or economics, even more so if they need a historical perspective. Design students, whether concentrating on industrial design or not, will find lots to interest and stimulate them here.

Folk museums
Folk museums, museums of rural life — they go under all sorts of names. What they all do in essence is to chart the lives and homes of ordinary people. They sometimes include shops, workshops, and reconstructions of real old buildings. Going round the best of these is just like travelling back in time. There is none of the 'museum' feeling about them — it really feels more like nosing round someone else's house or shop. The **Castle Museum** in York is one of the earliest of this type and still one of the best, but others exist now all over the country. Students of virtually every subject will find material to interest them and to spark off ideas and questions in their mind.

'Subject' museums
These are scattered all over the country but the greatest concentration is in the national museums in London. The **Natural History Museum**, the **Science Museum** and the **Victoria and Albert** are national collections of great importance to scholars. They put on major exhibitions and a visit to one of these can be an experience which stays with you and is really exciting and rewarding. If you live within reach of London, do make an effort

to visit these centres. But do not assume there is nothing like it for you if you live in the provinces. The **National Museum of Photography** in Bradford (an amazing collection — lots here for everyone even if you are not a camera buff) and the **Railway Museum** in York are two national museums not in London.

"I'm thinking of charging admission!"

Other museums

Museums are not always collections of inanimate objects. The **Newham Grange Farm** in Cleveland not only details old agricultural life in the area but also keeps and breeds various types of livestock seldom seen on modern farms. Museums are scattered all over the place and you may be surprised at what exists within say twenty miles of your home. I live in a very rural part of North Yorkshire but near me I have:

- A small museum in the local market town showing mainly Roman remains.
- A very good costume collection in a large country home about ten miles away.
- A folk museum about six miles distance concentrating on the lives of ordinary people.
- A fantastic museum of rural life covering many acres and with old cottages and houses rebuilt on the site and furnished with genuine old pieces. Places like this often have 'craft' days when experts come in and demonstrate many of the old crafts.
- A National Trust property in the next village which is a museum in itself.

Because museums have actual objects on show and concentrate on the visual impact they can often help to clear up or explain things that are difficult to grasp from a written description. Museums are often short of space, and so cannot show off everything. Ask the staff what else you can see.

NEWSPAPERS

All areas have a local paper of some sort and many of these have a very long publishing history. Until fairly recently it was quite common for even small towns to have two newspapers, and large cities often had a range of both morning and evening papers. This has changed now, though, and it is unusual to find more than one paper serving an area. Don't forget to check if others have existed in the past as files of these should still be available in your local library. The most obvious use for these will be local history. You can check on buildings, happenings and people in your area.

Back issues

If you live in the town where the paper is published then the office will hold all the **back copies** — otherwise ask in your nearest library. This is particularly important in the case of a newspaper which is no longer published. One problem with local papers is that they seldom have any sort of index to them. Go armed with as much prior information as possible, so that you can at least make an intelligent guess at the rough date you need. Some of the major national papers — in particular *The Times* publish very good indexes to their contents and in the case of *The Times* stretching back a very long way. They can sometimes help you pinpoint a special national event, battle, or celebration so that you then know where to look in your local paper.

A mirror of life

Never underestimate the value of papers for all sorts of things. They are mirrors of social history not only in what they have reported over the years but also in how they have reported it. Look at the fascinating job adverts, patent medicine claims, and reports of local firms and events. Economics, sociology, history, graphic design, business history, urban architecture — all are mirrored in the local paper.

Making crown glass — illustration from a Victorian magazine.

ART GALLERIES AND PICTURE LIBRARIES

Most large cities have an art collection of some sort but do not think of this as being purely pictures — sculpture and all sorts of other forms of art may be included. The best of them will have items of national importance as well as collections of local artists' work. Most of them will also have extensive **slide collections** — very useful if you cannot get to see the original. Remember that pictures are not just for the artist — they are histories of fashion, landscape and often interpreters of great national events.

Many art galleries will have a specialised **art library** as well. **Picture libraries** are a slightly different sort of resource — their main role is to collect pictures or illustrations from all sorts of places, index them and then either hire them or sell them to people who need a picture of a particular place, piece of machinery or anything else. Journalists, publishers and TV producers make a lot of use of these libraries but it is unlikely you will need their specialised services, which are also fairly expensive.

Popular books and magazines were a rich source of illustration in the nineteenth century (engraving showing paper-making by hand).

PRESS CUTTINGS

These really go hand in hand with newspaper libraries. They take the hard work out of searching in individual papers for people who need material on a topic and are prepared to pay for someone else to do the work. Most of these, such as Durrants, are commercial undertakings but you may be lucky and find that your local library keeps a cuttings file perhaps on local buildings. It could save you a lot of time.

RECORD OFFICES

Most large towns and all counties in England and Wales have a record office where all the old documents about the area will be kept. An **archivist** who is specially trained to preserve these very old papers, and to read and interpret them, will be in charge and prepared to help any member of the public.

One of the obvious things the record office holds is all the original papers to do with the history of the area, but it does not stop there. Records of families, firms and churches will also often be housed there as record offices try to make their collections as complete as possible. Much of this material dates from at least Elizabethan (Tudor) times and sometimes earlier. Remember that these are all original documents and often need a specialist to help in interpreting not only the meaning but also the old-fashioned style of writing as well. Their main use is for historical research and they are the primary sources from which many history books are written. If history is your subject, they are well worth a visit.

CHURCH RECORDS

Some of these may have been handed over to the local record office but many churches still have their own. The church **registers** are vital for anyone wanting to trace their family history, since they record all local marriages, christenings and funerals. Most vicars are only too happy to share their knowledge with you. The history of an area is very often closely tied to the history of the church so this resource is well worth remembering.

Church Libraries

At one time, most churches had their own libraries. In the Middle Ages they acted like the public library of today and provided religious manuscripts and books mainly for the very few, usually monks and priests, who could read. Some of these old libraries still exist and there are quite extensive collections particularly in cathedrals and large parish churches.

Book-binding by hand (about 1600).

Using other resources

COMPANY RECORDS

Many companies have very long histories — although what with takeovers and name changes this may not always be apparent. Most keep all their important records and some of the bigger ones such as Marks & Spencer have employed professional writers to write their history. Many of these will also act as histories of the particular technology involved, so can have more than one use.

Pamphlets and small booklets are quite often printed by a small firm to celebrate a centenary or other landmark. These are sometimes difficult to trace as they are often given away to valued clients, and not put on general sale. Hopefully the local library will receive a copy. Ask the firm concerned for help — most of them will be only too happy to give you the information you need.

CITIZENS ADVICE BUREAU (CAB)

Quite a different sort of resource from those mentioned earlier in this chapter but a most important and useful place to know about. All large towns have one of these open for most of the day, and even small places have one that operates on a part-time basis.

They aim to offer advice and help on all aspects of what you might call 'social law and legislation' — in other words, rents, housing, social security benefits, welfare payments, allowances of all sorts, and everything really to do with how the individual copes with official bodies. If you are not sure whether you qualify for a grant or are in a mess over a debt or some other problem, do go and talk to the CAB. They cannot solve the problem for you but can often help to smooth the path and put you in touch with someone who can help. If you are on any student course which demands a knowledge of social legislation, then some of the CAB publications could be very useful to you.

PEOPLE AS A RESOURCE

Never underestimate the value of what *people* can tell you. They have **experiences**, **anecdotes**, **memories** all of which can bring the past alive and help you to fill out and add to the printed word. People who have worked with particular machinery, in a local firm, fought in a war or lived in an area since demolished are all **primary sources** and should never be overlooked.

- *Tip* Never give up. *Somewhere* there will be the answer to your query. Keep on searching!

Special needs can be met in a record library, too.

7
Special Library Services

Libraries, as we have said, are not all that good at advertising themselves or their services. As well as the Lending and Reference departments, most libraries have all sorts of other facilities which are there for you to use — this chapter gives a run-down of the more common ones. All large public libraries should have at least some of these, and even small branches may have the odd extra tacked on.

Telephone directories
Even small branches will have telephone directories for the surrounding area. Bigger libraries will have not only all the ones for Great Britain but probably also at least some from Europe and the USA. These, with the yellow pages, are a fantastic source of information. Aside from individual addresses they include firms in a particular area, and can help you check your nearest Vauxhall dealer or garden centre. Telephone directories will probably be kept in the Reference area, but may be in the Commercial Library if there is one. If you are looking for a particular place in Britain and do not know which directory it will be in, make sure the **index** to the directories is there. It will save you hours of frustration.

Electors List
Every area has a list updated annually of all those people eligible to vote. This is issued in street order so you can check to see whether you are on it. Also, if needs be, you can discover who lives in a particular house. Post Offices also hold copies of this. Among the many people who consult electors lists are the police, and sales companies.

Local Diary
Most public libraries keep a diary in a prominent place, usually in the lending area, where local meetings and events are entered. You should also be able to find out the names and addresses of local secretaries of **clubs and societies** from the library.

Tourist information

In some places, the local tourist office is housed under the same roof as the library. This is usually packed with leaflets, maps, guides, and entertainment brochures — all dealing with the local area. The staff are specially trained to help tourists. Details of accommodation are also available here although this is usually aimed at the short-term visitor rather than the permanent resident. Even if the tourist office is located elsewhere, the library will still have a certain amount of information and can certainly guide you to the best source for your needs. Additionally many public libraries hold copies of all the **town guides** for tourists and holiday-makers.

Official leaflets and information

Libraries are usually on the mailing list for all the official leaflets put out by bodies like the **DHSS** the **Department of Employment** and the **Inland Revenue**. Most libraries have a special place to display these, but if you cannot see them, do ask. You may find a librarian whose job it is to look after all these and help you to understand them. They will certainly be able to tell you where to go for more specialised help.

Music and records

The larger public libraries nearly all have **record libraries** and often lend **sheet music** as well. You may have to pay a small subscription or deposit to join this but it does mean you will have access to a large collection and not by any means all 'classical' either. Ask the librarian if you can have a browse around before you join so that you have some idea of what is on offer.

Play and choir sets

Large libraries will often have multiple copies of plays or sets of music to lend out to amateur societies. If you are in a college or youth group, it makes sense to see what you can borrow for free before making your choice. Special arrangements are made for **extended loans** for these sets.

Video library

These are still relatively rare but are growing in number. They operate much like the record libraries; you may have to pay to join and also possibly pay a small amount for each video you borrow. This will vary from one library to another, so always ask. Remember, too, to check which video system you have — will the library videos be compatible?

Special library services

Patents
Every time someone invents something new, they take out a **patent** on it. This means that no-one else may copy that idea and get the credit for it (or the financial benefit). The patent is printed with all the details of the invention, including technical drawings, and major libraries will keep copies of all these. This is a very specialised part of the library and needs highly trained staff who understand the whole field. It is not very likely that you will need to look up a patent but if you do, go to the nearest large public library and ask for the **patent librarian**.

Exhibition collections
Some libraries collect books on a particular topic, or for a special age-group or purpose, and keep them together as a **special collection** which may not be broken up or lent out. This is useful if you need to see a wide range of books on the same topic. Much will depend on how your library feels about this sort of collection as some librarians prefer their books to be loaned rather than 'locked up' in exhibitions.

Quite often you will find that a local benefactor has left his own specialised collection to the library; this is often kept separately.

Local history collections
Public libraries have always seen themselves as being guardians of any material to do with the town or surrounding area. Often the bigger libraries employ a specialised librarian to look after this and to help enquirers find their answers. These collections can be full of fascinating material (not all of it old and dead by any means).

Large print books and other specialised aids
Many people of all ages have problems with their eyes and all libraries now stock a range of books with large print specially to help with this. You should be able to find something to suit all tastes, but of course the range is limited and nothing like as great as the choice of normal print size. In the main, you will find that large print books are aimed more at the recreational reader (especially fiction) and it is more difficult to find books for study purposes in large print.

Some libraries are now starting to put in **deaf loops** as well as providing things like **magnifiers**, **reading machines** and other special aids. **Access ramps** are becoming more common and increasingly it is becoming easier for everyone regardless of particular problems, to use the library. If you or any of your friends, fall into this category, then do make enquiries about what services exist to help. Many large libraries have special **mobile services** that visit people in their homes if they are unable to reach the library and staff specially trained to help.

Teenage libraries

Libraries are often at a loss where to put books aimed specifically at this age group. Not surprisingly, most teenagers do not want to go on using the children's library, but on the other hand, the books most appealing to them would get 'lost' on the adult shelves. The solution some libraries have adopted is to house all these books together, often with some study space as well, sympathetic staff and friendly and welcoming atmosphere. You may be lucky to find such a service in your town. Teenagers in Bradford, for example, have a special room complete with computer games, pop magazines and a selection of board games as well as comfy chairs and a relaxed atmosphere.

Larger college libraries and public libraries should have all of these:

Foreign language books

Most libraries will have some books in foreign languages, but what there is will depend on two things;

- the sort of library it is and who it serves and
- the area in which you live.

If you are in a large college where languages are an important part of the curriculum then you will probably find a large stock of whatever is studied. All larger public libraries will have books in the main European languages including French, German, Italian, Spanish and so on.

However, if you live in an area where many people from abroad have settled, then the choice is likely to be much wider. Polish, Greek, all the Indian languages will be there together with others that are represented in your community. Obviously these are of great benefit to native speakers but can also be interesting and useful to students. At one time only the 'classics' in the various languages would be stocked but that is no longer true; a wide selection should be on the shelves. If you are just learning a language then the books aimed at children may come in very useful as the words and grammar are usually fairly simple and easy to understand.

Maps

Big libraries hold very comprehensive stocks of all the **Ordnance Survey** maps as well as lots of tourist maps and many specialised historical, geological and other subject maps. They will also have all the different scales of maps for their own area including the very large scale that shows individual houses and streets. You should be able to pinpoint your own home. You should also find **street maps** to the major cities and also a good collection of **overseas maps**, although some of these may not be for loan.

Illustrations collections
Some libraries keep folders of pictures, often just cut out of local papers and magazines and kept in rough subject order. They can be helpful if you need an illustration of an old object or piece of machinery, for example, but unless they are very well organised (a very time consuming task) they are sometimes not much use. Some college libraries operate a 'bring-one-take-one' system. In other words you can take a picture from the collection providing you bring one to add to the total.

Photocopying
Most libraries, particularly colleges, offer copying facilities at a reasonable price. However, don't forget the **copyright laws** — they lay down very strict rules about what and how much you can copy, and for what purposes. If in doubt, ask the librarian.

College libraries and bigger school libraries should have all of these:

Examination papers
Whatever examination boards are used in your college, you should find samples of past papers in the library. It has been known for lecturers to hang on to these, so if you cannot find them, always ask.

Computer programs
As more and more teaching and learning becomes computer-orientated, college libraries are stocking more and more programs. Sometimes you may only use these in the library (but a computer will be provided for you to use) but you may be able to borrow some. These can be very useful as revision aids or to give you a step-by-step breakdown of a process or problem.

Tapes and cassettes
Much educational material is found on sound tapes and college libraries will always stock some of these at least. They are very good for languages, literature and music — in fact anything where what you hear is more important than what you see. Again, some libraries will have proper **study carrels** with the appropriate machinery for you to use in the library.

Educational videos
Although some public libraries now have video libraries of mainly recreational material, colleges will almost always concentrate on ones produced specifically to help students. There is now a very large range of these; they are gradually replacing the old film-strip and even the slide set.

Slides and film strips
Not so popular as they were, really because of the growth of video, but they still have their uses, particularly slides.

Open University material
Although this is all prepared for students studying for OU degrees much of it has spin-offs for people doing all sorts of other exams. It is usually very clear and concise and it is well worth finding out what there is available in your subject. Many college libraries buy Open University material even if there is no link with the Open University in that college.

Distance learning material
This is a fairly new concept and you may not always find it in your college library. It is really a development (although much more sophisticated) of the old idea of learning by correspondence courses. Distance learning, though, has complete **learning packages** which include *all* the material you would need to learn a particular topic or skill. Again, very useful for reinforcement and revision as well as for the beginner in a subject.

● *Tip* All libraries of whatever sort, large or small, are supermarkets of information. Make sure you know what *your* library contains.

Libraries have always been leaders in the use of information technology.

8
The Information Revolution

THE INFORMATION REVOLUTION

There are still plenty of people around who think of libraries as quiet, oak-panelled rooms, with old-fashioned staff, no talking and nothing else but leather-bound tomes on the shelves.

If you look very hard, you might find the very old scholarly society library that still retains this image, but most libraries today are in the forefront of some of the newest techniques for information searching. Indeed, librarians are some of the most 'switched on' and expert professionals when it comes not only to computer use but also the whole range of **teletext**, **video**, **terminals**, **CCTV** and all the other jargon words connected with this field you can think of.

Its beginnings in libraries

Strangely enough (to most people who are not librarians, anyway) librarians have had a long history of computer involvement. They were experienced and expert in this field long before the craze hit the general public. Nearly all the large public, university and polytechnic libraries have been using computers for a very long time, both for 'housekeeping' jobs like recording who has borrowed what, printing overdue notices and files of books on order, and also for **information retrieval**.

The computerised routine jobs will not really affect the borrower to any extent — their biggest spin-off for you is that they may give the library staff more time to help with reader queries.

The whole field of information technology though, is one any serious student needs to get to grips with. It encompasses all the machinery of hardware which use the new microchip technologies. Not only do they store information, they communicate it to others on either perhaps a restricted basis just for students in one college, or at the other extreme to allow you access to a worldwide **database** with thousands of pieces of information stored in one system.

Modern information systems

How do these systems work? Let's take the large information, or database, systems first. Scattered over the world are very large computers all holding massive amounts of information. Most of this information will be rather like the abstracts and indexes we discussed earlier. The big difference here is that not only can a single search provide references to years and years back (instead of manually having to look at each volume); it can also bring together lots of separate abstracts or indexes so saving an incredible amount of search time. The advantages of these bases are many.

Speed

Most of the major abstracts and indexes are now held on computer bases and some you can only get on computer as they are not printed in book form any more. By selecting the **key words** for your topic, you can have a selection of appropriate references in minutes (often less). Contrast that with having to work through many printed volumes of each individual abstract.

Usually you will have a VDU in front of you to see what the computer comes up with, but most of these large computer systems also have a **printout** facility and if you are prepared to wait a few days for the post, you can have a printed record of everything the computer has found.

Worldwide network

These databases mean that, providing your library has a terminal, you can be linked up to a worldwide information network. No longer do you have to do all your work in one of the very large libraries with massive stocks. Even small college or school libraries can now provide facilities and services for their borrowers undreamed of a few years ago.

Wider choice

Your choice of services and your access to information is now probably wider than it would be in any library in the world with the possible exception of places like the British Museum library or the Library of Congress in Washington.

More information

More and more information of all sorts is now available on computer, or through computer links. It's a good thing for everyone — not just students — to learn how to get the best out of these systems. Students now have a huge built-in advantage in that much of their education has introduced them to computers for all sorts of topics. But remember, searching for information is a very skilled business and playing games on computers is no real training for this. You may be able to drive a car but competing in the Monte Carlo rally demands special techniques. Learn the computer techniques early on in your student career and they will stand you in good stead.

There are however some disadvantages to these massive databases:

The cost
Many of these computer databases are in the United States: as the connection between your computer and the American one is by telephone, you can soon appreciate how the phone bills can mount up. This cost factor often forces libraries to impose limits on *who* can access these databases and for *how long* — they usually have to foot the bill so do not want money wasted by inexperienced searchers or people just fooling around.

Staff time
Many libraries now have staff whose role it is to help borrowers with computer searches and perhaps do them for them.

Most of these databases have a manual to help with the task but many of them are, like much computer 'literature', difficult for the layperson to understand, so you often need help from an expert. This means that in some busy research libraries, staff may have little time for anything else but carrying out computer searches for their borrowers. Contrast this

"I think there's a malfunction in search mode."

CHECKLIST FOR A SEARCH	
1. What do I need to know?	How does the price of coffee affect the Third World?
2. What **key** words describe that accurately?	Coffee. Third World.
3. Do I need to add any other **key** words to make sure I only get articles of use to my project and not ones about growing coffee in the third world?	Add *Economy*.
4. How far back in time do I need to go?	The project is to do with the present situation so two years back will be enough to show the background and give a comparative view.
5. Is it better to choose a computer search, or use printed abstracts?	Unless you are very experienced and knowledgeable, you will probably need to ask your librarian or your lecturer.
6. Where can I read any of the articles or books that the search produces?	If you are not sure, ask the librarian.
7. Will I have to pay anything for a computer search?	Unlikely if you are in any sort of academic library, but check if you are using a public library.

with using conventional printed sources — the librarian here may spend perhaps a quarter of an hour showing a borrower what is available and how to find it, but that is enough to let you get on by yourself — not only on that occasion but for subsequent searches as well. Libraries which are short of staff (nearly all of them!) can find that doing computer searches places a very heavy burden on top of everything else they must do.

Charges

If you are using these facilities in a college, university or polytechnic library, then for you it will probably be a free service. However, some public libraries are under increasing pressure to charge extra for computer searches, at least to cover the cost of any phone calls. Opinions are divided over the rights and wrongs of this, but as you may be asked to pay make sure what the situation is before you ask for a lengthy computer session.

Serendipity

Serendipity means making helpful or interesting discoveries by accident. It's an odd thing, but often when you are looking for some information, you can come across it quite by accident. Despite all the rules you have followed, and the care you have taken to define what you need, it does sometimes happen that you find just what you need in spite of all this and not because of it!

It often happens when you are consulting an index, abstract or even periodical for one thing and quite by chance your eye lights on something else. It really comes back to the browsing round the shelves tip, though here it is printed sources you are 'browsing' through. With computer searches you cannot do this so you may sometimes miss important clues.

Getting the answer you want

The computer search will, very rarely, give you the answer to your query but what it *will* give you is a list of references, usually in periodicals, on your chosen topic. This means that you still have the job of tracking down the individual periodicals, or books, so you need access to a good library or one where it is fairly easy for them to borrow material for you.

Remember these computer databases are expanding at a tremendous rate — more topics are included, more abstracting and indexing services computerised and the range of information available growing each day.

● *Tip* Keep in touch with what is happening in your subject and make the best use of what exists.

Only by learning as much as you can will you be able to judge when a printed source is more use to you than a computerised one. Don't make the mistake of thinking that just because it's 'high tech' it is always better than the older and more conventional ways: they have their uses, too!

"I asked the computer for a list of the works of Plato, but got a list of self-catering holidays in Greece!"

School and college computers
If you are in a fairly large college, then you may find that as well as having access to the larger computer databases, you also can use small **microcomputers** holding specific information relevant to particular courses or topics. Most educational establishments are now littered with computers, but it is still not all that common to find one in the library, and this is specially true of school libraries. If you are one of the lucky ones, you may find your library has a micro with a database listing everything the library contains on say pollution or old age, or other topics where the information is scattered and not easy to track down. Remember, though, that these small computers are restricted in the amount they can hold so they cannot cope with very large databases and are not nearly so flexible as their bigger brothers.

However, there seems little doubt that storing information in this way will increase — and as computers become more sophisticated, then the range of what they can do will also grow.

- Data stored in this way takes up very little space
- It can be accessed by anyone who can type with one finger
- It can be shared with other libraries or enquirers over a wide area by means of a telephone link.

If you are in a school or college on a split site, you may find that a micro is already being used to overcome some of the physical problems of two buildings.

Unless you have a **minicomputer** or **mainframe** in your college, you are not likely to find all the library catalogue on your micro — it just will not have the capacity for that. It may have booklists, though, perhaps a database on further and higher education available locally, or any other topic that is in demand and not easy to obtain by other means.

Micros in college libraries are ideal for learning all about search techniques on computer. Once mastered, these same principles can be applied to the bigger international databases, but at least you can get some simple practice in first. It is also most unlikely that you will be asked to pay for using a small computer in your school or college — being able to use a computer effectively is seen as a positive learning experience, and you will be encouraged to make the most of what is on offer in the information technology field.

Television
It is odd to think that the ordinary TV set in the corner of the living room has the potential to be a very important information source. But it already has the ability to be talked 'at' and give you answers.

Most people will have seen the **Oracle** transmissions on ITV and the **Ceefax** ones on BBC — the bits of written text you find on the screen between programmes, bringing you up-to-date on travel news, weather forecasts as well as odd snippets of other information. They are really aimed to whet your appetite and tantalise those of us who do not have the specially adapted **teletext** sets which would let us see all this written information.

If you do have one of these sets, then you get a **key pad** with it (rather like a remote control pad). With that you can literally 'turn the pages' and select what information you want to read. Just key in the appropriate page number and up pops what you want.

Prestel

Prestel is really a more sophisticated development of this idea. It's more expensive and needs a telephone connected to it to work, so you usually find these TV sets in libraries, offices and other more commercial places. Prestel contains a very wide range of information. Much of it, like stock market prices, is updated very quickly.

Some businesses, like the travel trade, make great use of Prestel. As well as the information on it that anyone can use, it is possible to have a private **network** that only certain people can use. Travel agencies use a private network to do much of their bookings and other firms with offices scattered nationwide can also use a private network to keep all their staff up-to-date on new product information or new prices.

It does cost quite a lot to use Prestel. We are back to the telephone cost to a certain extent, since all the information actually comes down the phone line although it is shown on the screen. Some of the 'pages' on Prestel also carry a special charge and if you want to see that page, you will be charged for it. Like the Ceefax and Oracle sets you have a key pad and can 'talk' to your set through that.

If your college or school has Prestel, you may be able to use it quite freely, since all educational establishments have a cheaper rate, but even so you may find some rules and regulations to keep the cost down. If you are on a business studies course or a travel trade one, then the chances are that familiarising yourself with Prestel will be part of your syllabus and your teacher will introduce you to what is on offer. You do not necessarily need a TV set to access Prestel — a computer with telephone link works just as well. With the correct software package, it is quite easy to produce your own **viewdata** service, tailored specifically to local needs.

You may find your college is part of a **network** providing a wide range of information for all the students in a geographical area. If you have the chance, get involved yourself in helping with this. All computer work is a classic example of 'learning by doing' so any experience is bound to help.

Interactive video

Video in all its various forms is likely to figure in the college library as a positive teaching medium. It is now possible to have **interactive video** where by touching the screen you can alter the picture. This is very useful in technical training when complicated drawings or perhaps machinery can be displayed and students encouraged to 'repair' faults or spot potential problems. The video can then respond to the student's solution and quickly correct the wrong response. These machines can be very useful if you embark on any self-programming course.

CAL

Computer assisted learning in a way relies on the same techniques as the interactive video. The computer software offers you certain options and will not let you go on to the next bit until you key in the correct answer. This is again very useful for both revision and for students who have to work away from a teacher.

Technically speaking, all the machines mentioned in this chapter can be hooked up to each other and used in a variety of ways. Often it is only lack of money that stops a college or school from providing much more of this information technology. You may be lucky and find all sorts of exciting things going on in your school or college — much will depend on the enthusiasm of the librarian and other staff.

> ● *Tip* Learn all you can about all these developments. Anyone who hopes to get on now has to be **computer-literate** and that means much more than just being able to play computer games.

9
The Librarian's Day

7.30 a.m.
Roll out of bed, put kettle on, get washed. Kick everyone else out and try to get organised for the mad rush. It never seems to get any better but at least after two cups of coffee I start to feel slightly more human.

8.15 a.m.
It's a miserable wet, windy day and I wait at the bus-stop praying that the bus arrives soon.

8.50 a.m.
Get to work and check who else has arrived. For once it seems all the staff are here and there are no panics over who can cover the lunch period or work late.

9.00 a.m.
Jane, our senior library assistant, unlocks the main library door and we are open for 'business' once more. The library counter staff, all three of them, are busy getting ready for the new day. Jane has already altered the date stamp for books taken out, Judith is sorting out books that are reserved for someone else and Martin has his list organised for books that are due back from the short-loan collect. (In our library college students may borrow some of the most heavily used books overnight but have to bring them back first thing in the morning. Execution awaits those who fall down on this rule — or at least a refusal to lend them anything else!)

Jane, Judith and Martin all have their own particular parts of the shelves to keep tidy and in order, as well as shelving all the return books, so they will take it in turns through the day to get those jobs done. As long as someone is always on the counter, they can sort out that for themselves.

9.10 a.m.

Kath, our library assistant who looks after the periodicals, has sorted out the new ones into their 'subject' piles. I am responsible for all the Maths and Computing side of our library so this means that not only are all the students doing these subjects my responsibility if they need any library help, but also much of the book selection is under my wing — although of course, many of the suggestions come from the lecturing staff.

I spend my next half-hour skimming through the new periodicals for articles of interest to any other teaching staff and for reviews and details of new books. I keep a list of useful articles I find and these can often help with a student problem. All the teaching staff find it useful to have a quick flip through my cards. If I find anything particularly important, I send a note to the member of staff concerned so that they do not miss it. I have a quick look at my 'books to order file' — this seems to be growing at an alarming rate; I suspect we shall run out of money before I get to the end of it. It's one of the problems of working in this subject area that the information changes very rapidly and new books are produced at a terrific rate. Trying to keep up with it all is a mammoth task as well as being a very expensive one, too.

10.00 a.m.

Am beginning to gasp for coffee but before I can have that, I have a spell on the enquiry desk. Each of the professional librarians (there are three of us here) take it in turns to sit and work out in the library with a big sign on the desk saying *Enquiries*. Some days you can get on well with your own work (I usually take some book reviews or periodical I want to catch up on) but other times it can seem like Piccadilly Circus with students milling around with all sorts of problems.

When you are on the 'desk' you have to be prepared to help students doing all sorts of courses, not just in your own subject area. This keeps you on your toes and makes sure you do not lose touch with what the rest of the college is doing.

My first question was, 'Where are the history books?' If they were all like that, this would be a cushy number but my next student was on a business studies course and had to do a project on Travelling Salesmen. This entailed much talk to the student about what she had already found, and where, what gaps she had to fill and where we might find what she needed. It involved me in teaching her how to use abstracts and indexes as she had not come across these before, and even after she had gone off to do her own searching, I kept popping back to make sure she was not in a mess and still on the right track.

My next enquiry was quite different — a nursery nurse student going out into local day nurseries and wanting some suitable stories to read to her young charges. Luckily, this is a personal interest of mine so she and I spent a happy twenty minutes looking at books and discussing the value of story with young children. I was quite overcome when she said she had learned more from me than her lecturer!

11.00 a.m.
Coffee at last — meet half the library staff in the staff room. The other half had their break earlier. One of the problems of working in a library is that you hardly ever see the staff altogether (apart from the Christmas dinner, that is).

When you are 'off' someone else has to be 'on'. Libraries are a little like the old Windmill Theatre — 'We never close'. Sit and relax for quarter of an hour — discuss last night's abysmal TV with Michael (one of the other professional librarians who looks after Social Sciences) and Jane and Kath. Catch up on the saga of Jane's love-life and forget all about work for a while.

11.15 a.m.
Michael and I have a short meeting with Liz, the Chief Librarian. We have to sort out the holiday rotas for a start. This is always a tricky problem as most of us have young children so really want time off during the school holidays.

Although all the students, and many of the staff, disappear at the end of term, we keep on working through and manage to catch up on a lot of jobs that are impossible to fit in during term-time.

We also have to discuss a proposed student teaching programme for next term. Michael and I have roughed out a programme of lessons on how to use the library more effectively, but now have to get down to the detail. We need to liaise with all the subject departments so that we can tie in with what the students have to do for their course work. We realised long ago that it was no use doing this unless we could make the students see how it could help them in their studies. Now we go to great lengths to try to make sure each of our courses is tailored to the relevant subject areas.

12.00 a.m.
One of the computing lecturers turns up unexpectedly to tell me that his course is likely to alter its content next year. This will very much affect the book and periodical stock so I abandon my checking of new editions and he and I discuss the implications for the library in any change of syllabus. It will mean quite a lot of extra work in both identifying new titles, and in withdrawing ones that are of no further use.

It also has financial implications. Knowing that, as usual, we are chronically short of money, I wonder how Liz will react to this new demand on our straitened resources.

I suggest to Ken that he might ask the Academic Board for a special grant to cover new books and materials for his course as this has often been granted in the past. However, the college as a whole is short of money so we may not be so lucky this time.

12.30 p.m.
Lunch-time. Toss a mental coin between our rather grotty refectory or the staff common-room. The latter is more comfortable but only serves coffee and sandwiches whereas the refectory at least has a choice of hot and cold meals (never have the moussaka though — heaven knows what's in it). I plump for the refectory and treat myself to sausage and chips — nice and warming on a cold day.

Find lots of other staff in there and join a group of lecturers. We all have a good moan about how awful everything is and how badly we are all treated. Always useful to have a chance to talk to other members of staff — sometimes the librarians can feel cut off from their teaching colleagues so anything that breaks this down is a good thing. We all sit on our appropriate subject committees in the college but Liz also encourages us to get involved in other things, too. Michael is a leading light on the Sports Committee whilst I am a member of the Social group that organises staff outings and parties.

1.30 p.m.
Back to the grindstone. Michael is on the Enquiry desk, which leaves me free to get on in the back — hopefully without disturbance. Librarianship is one job where you can never really stick to a rigid timetable. You never know what interruptions you may get or what sudden queries you may be faced with. It's one of the charms of the work for me and certainly never allows you to get bored or stale, and keeps you on your toes.

However, I have promised the Head of Computing to do a computer literature search for him so want to get that done now if possible. He wants to know what has been published on farmers who may be using expert systems to diagnose crop diseases. He suspects that little work has been done on this and thinks there may be a chance of a research project here for his advanced students.

This is a tricky problem and involves me in a lot of work before I even reach the computer terminal. Our college has a link to the Dialog computer database in the United States but it is very expensive to use so I must make sure before I start that I am asking the computer the right questions and using all the correct 'key words'. I start with the manuals supplied with the Dialog terminal and decide to access first the Dialindex — in other words the index to all the Dialog databases. I make a list of terms or 'key words' which should throw up useful references and then combine them so that the search I decide on will, hopefully, catch any relevant articles.

I choose crop diseases, expert systems and hand-held computers as my three index words. (I chose the latter as I understand from the lecturer and my own reading that these computers are now taken into fields by the farmers with the appropriate program in them so that they can identify on the spot what the trouble might be!)

This is a fairly lengthy process and I am still not at the terminal. However, it is vital to do this preliminary work thoroughly otherwise two equally disastrous happenings occur — firstly you miss important references because you have not thought out your search strategy logically or clearly, and secondly you spend far more money than is necessary and suffer the wrath not only of the librarian but also the College Bursar who finally has to foot the bill.

All this early work is rewarded since the actual time spent linked up to the States is relatively short. I discover that not very much work has been done in this area at all so there may be a good research project waiting for someone to tackle. I arrange for a printout of all the relevant articles to be sent — you can go through them all on the VDU but this means much more time linked up so it is much cheaper to get a printout of all the references sent on. Even so, this has cost the college around £20 but this is still cheap when you think how long it would take in staff time to do a search like this manually with abstracts and indexes.

There is no way, either, that a college library (or even some of the university libraries) would subscribe to all the sources necessary so it would be impossible to do except by using these computer databases.

3.00 p.m.
Tea-time. Liz is at a Curriculum Studies meeting this afternoon, so Michael and I are sharing the enquiry desk. It will be my stint again after tea.

3.15 p.m.
Take the draft of the new *User Guide* with me to the desk in the hope that I can do some work on it. Each year we update our library guide for new students but this year we have decided to try to produce slightly different ones for different subjects and different abilities.

Our college has nearly 3,000 students and they vary from 16 year olds doing O Levels to much older students doing almost degree-level work. What they need from the library varies tremendously so we thought we should try and tailor our service to each group much more specifically.

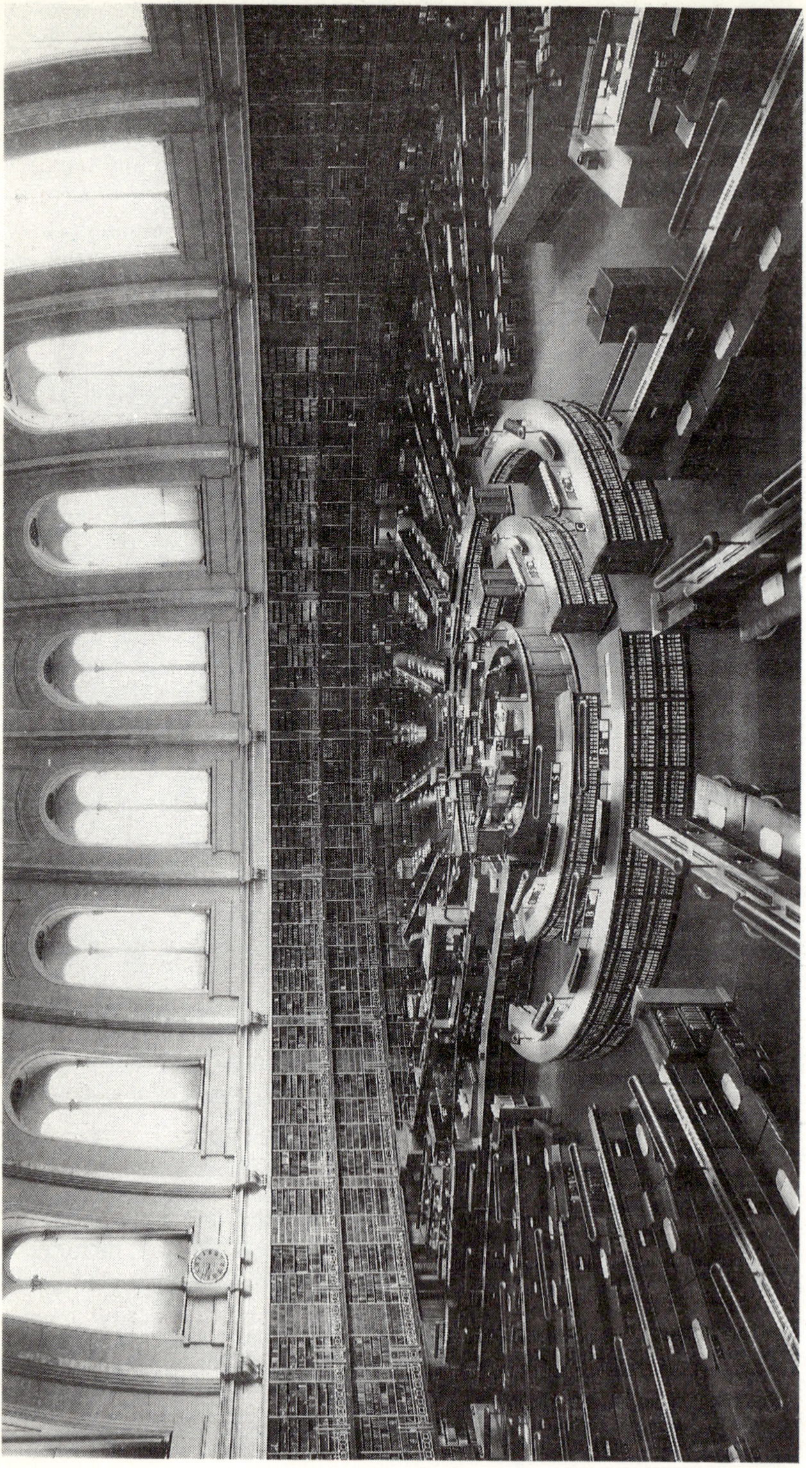

Left The famous circular Reading Room of the British Library in London, which contains a copy of almost every book published in Britain in modern times.
Serving the needs of the smaller community . . . *Above* A modern mobile library. *Below* A local high street library.

Above Children enjoying their library in Exmouth, Devon. *Below* A popular branch library. *Right* A well laid out lending library.

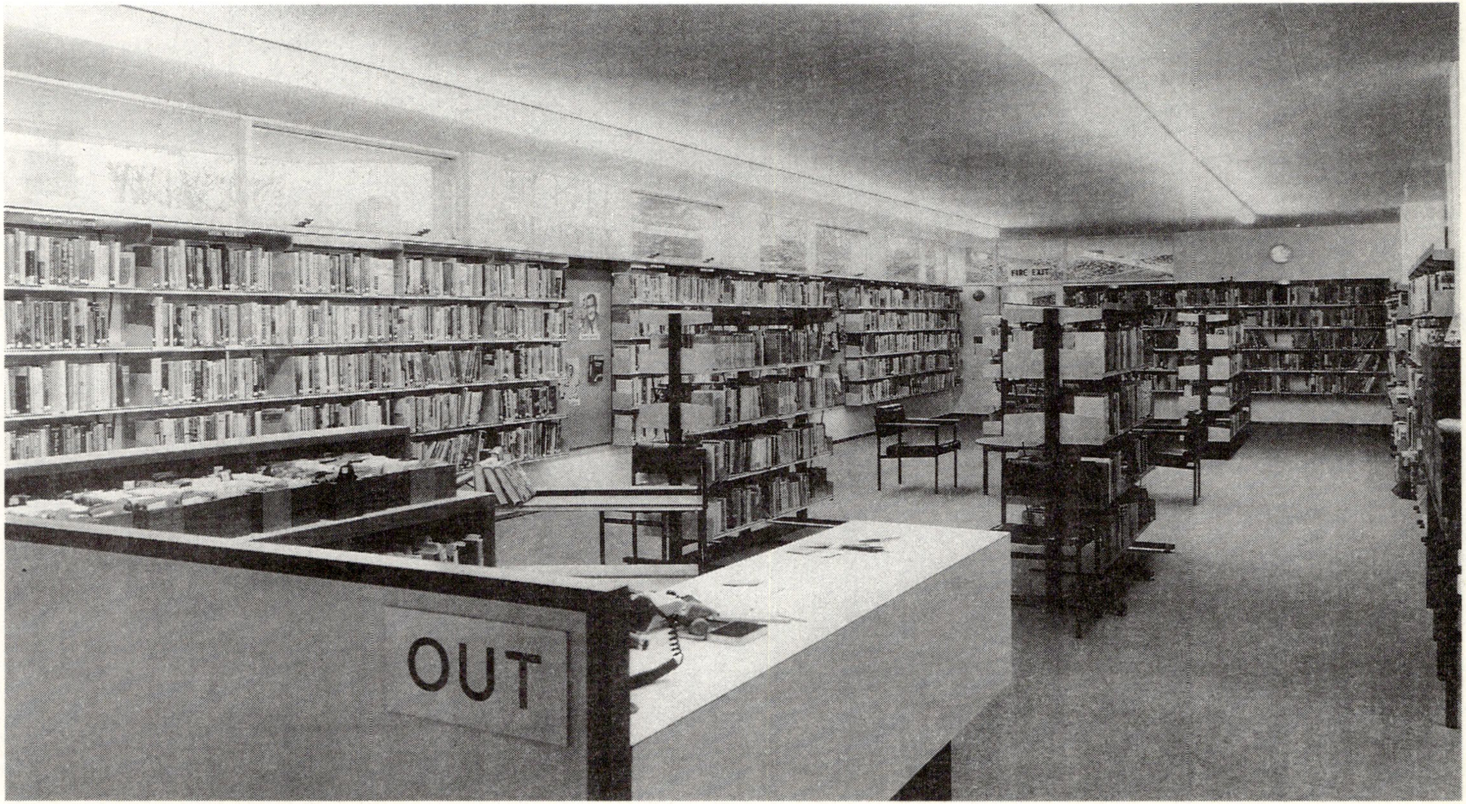
OUT
FIRE EXIT

This means a lot more work for us initially, but if we can get it right it should not only help the students much more but also indirectly all the library staff, as so many more 'enquirers' will be able to help themselves. I manage to have a quite peaceful time on the desk and get a lot of my own work done.

A first-year student asks me for help with the slide viewer and I make a mental note to do something about the instructions for this — there is still far too much 'jargon' about it and I am not surprised he could not work it. Liz returns from her meeting and relieves me for the last hour.

4.00 p.m.
Martin and I look at the short-loan list for Maths and Computing. I am sure some of these books could return to the ordinary shelves now and be loaned normally. Teaching staff are always very keen to have books put into this category but often forget to tell us when they can come off. Make a note of ones that seem 'surplus' and spend the next half-hour trying to track down the lecturers concerned. In the last analysis, I shall put the books back on the shelves myself if the teachers do not contact me.

4.30 p.m.
Beginning to wind down now (thank heavens it's not my late night — that's tomorrow). Sally, from the Computing Department, pops in to tell me about the next project her students will be doing. It will involve quite a bit of literature searching, some of it on the computer terminal, so she and I go through what the library can offer and how we should approach it.

It's always a difficult line to draw to know how far to help students with their work. Sometimes it is much easier and quicker to do the work yourself, but this is often not in the best interests of the student. It is always useful to discuss with the teaching staff concerned what their learning objectives are for each project.

5.00 p.m.
Home-time. Tidy up the chaos I seem to have made — give Liz my revised draft of the *User Guide*, wish Michael a peaceful evening (he is here until 8.00 p.m. with Jane and Martin) and rush for my bus.

10
Some Important Libraries in Britain

Public, school and college libraries have been the main ones discussed in this book, and they are the the ones you will always use the most. But there are lots of other sorts of libraries that you may need, and in your future career you may need to know more about these more specialised services. The list in this chapter is by no means comprehensive, but it tries to give you some idea of the range and also to show you that these are by no means all in London. There are directories of libraries and most large reference libraries will have copies of these, so if you are interested to find what exists near to you, ask to look in one of these. You may be surprised by what you find.

The British Library
This is an all-embracing title which includes a large number of individual libraries all doing slightly different things. Some of these are:

(a) **The Department of Printed Books**, Great Russell Street, London WC1B 3DG. This has existed since 1757 when George II presented the Royal Library to form the nucleus of the collection. As well as the actual books, there also come the important **copyright deposit** privileges. This meant (and still does mean) that one copy of every book published in Britain has to be deposited in the library. In 1823 a further gift was made of the library of George III so this ensured not only the growth of the collection but also its increasing importance. There are lots of specialised collections in here now ranging from the **Garrick Collection** of plays to **Sir Joseph Banks' Library** of botanical and zoological books to some of the oldest printed documents and manuscripts in the world. There are four open exhibition areas but if you want to be able to use the famous **Reading Room** and the full library facilities you have to apply for a readers' ticket.

(b) **The Science Reference Library**, 9 Kean Street, Drury Lane, London WC2, and 25 Southampton Buildings, Holborn, London WC2. This is the largest public scientific and technological reference library in Britain and it is also the national library for **patents**, **trademarks** and **designs**. There are two branches (both in London) with the one at Holborn concentrating on the inventive sciences like engineering, industrial technologies and commerce, and the Drury Lane Library having responsibility for all the life sciences, medicine and so on.

(c) **The Document Supply Centre**, Boston Spa, Wetherby, LS23 7BQ. This is the largest library in the world devoted to the supply of documents for loan, either by sending photocopies of what is requested or by lending the original document. It has a huge collection of periodicals from all over the world, as well as lots of books, and anyone may, through their own local pubic library, borrow anything from here. There is also a pleasant reading room that anyone can use.

There are lots of other libraries within the British Library and if you want to find out more, then you could write to any of these addresses or go to your nearest public library and ask for further information.

Wales and Scotland

Both Wales and Scotland have their own national libraries. The **National Library of Wales** is in Aberystwyth and it was opened in 1909. Like the British Library, it too is given one copy of every book published but it also has, quite naturally, a very large collection of books in Welsh and a unique library of very early Welsh books.

The **National Library of Scotland** is in Edinburgh. This is a much older foundation than the Welsh library; it began in 1682 as the library of the Faculty of Advocates. It became a copyright library as early as 1710 and so rapidly became a very important source. However, it did not actually become the National Library of Scotland until 1925 but today it is one of the four largest libraries in the UK.

Government Libraries

Government Libraries exist for all the major departments of the government and are there to serve the needs of the people who work there. Examples of these sorts of libraries are: The **Department of Employment Library** which has a large collection mainly dealing with industrial relations, working conditions, management and so forth, whilst the **Customs and Excise Departmental Library** contains information on indirect taxation as well as public finance and administration. Many of these government libraries are in London but you may be lucky to find one near to you.

Semi-government bodies (or **quangos** as they are sometimes called) also often have good libraries. The **Highlands and Islands Development Board** in Inverness has a good library covering such diverse subjects as rural development, tourism, off-shore gas and oil and fishing. The **Equal Opportunities Commission** in Manchester holds all the material on legislation to do with this subject, sociology, feminism, employment records, and also a collection of novels by women. There is also a section devoted to non-book material like cassettes and posters.

The **House of Commons Library** in Westminster is really a private research library for all the MPs and the library staff there spend a lot of time providing facts and figures to answer all sorts of queries. It takes over 1,700 periodicals and has a stock of around 133,000 books.

Charitable organisations

Charitable bodies or organisations set up to promote particular viewpoints will nearly always have libraries. **The Royal Society for the Prevention of Accidents** (RoSPA) in Birmingham covers all the necessary legislation, health and safety measures as well as details of all prosecutions in this field. Likewise, the **Health Education Council** in London is a very good source of information on everything from the dangers of smoking to health-care diets. Charities like the **Royal National Institute for the Blind** have a long history of library provision and act not only as collectors of all the sources of information on their particular subject but also provide a very good information service for everyone.

The **Disabled Living Foundation** provides an extremely good information service; it is always worth trying to find an organisation that covers your own interests as you may find the staff and service they provide answer all your queries.

The **Zoological Society of London** (or the London Zoo as most of us know it) also has a very good specialised collection on zoology but that is reserved for the use of the members of the society.

Research bodies

Research associations — groups of firms all working in the same field, who between them fund an information and library service they all can use — are important specialised centres of information. The **British Leather Manufacturers Research Association** in Leatherhead, Surrey, is basically there for the trade but anyone interested could ask to use their library.

These sorts of libraries are dotted all over the country — it's always worth finding out what exists near to you.

Industrial libraries.
Most large industrial firms have very good libraries, often built up over a long period. **Boots** in Nottingham has a large library used extensively by all its own research workers but also open to anyone who can show a need to use it. The library of **GEC Power Engineering** in Leicester has a really comprehensive collection on all aspects of engineering but with an emphasis on nuclear engineering.

State-owned industries, too, have very good libraries. The **National Coal Board** in London has over 40,000 books and 800 periodicals on all aspects of the coal industry. The **BBC** has a marvellous spread of libraries providing not only a current affairs service to all its staff but also probably the best record library in the country.

Places like the **Design Council** in London also have their own sources but in this case it is rather unusual as all their records are on 350,000 transparencies covering interiors, graphics, furniture and so on.

Provincial libraries
Don't feel that if you live out of London there is nothing near to you. How about the **Institute of Terrestrial Ecology** at Grange-over-Sands in Cumbria, or the **Shirley Institute of Textiles** in Manchester? Don't forget, either, the **Street Shoe Museum** in Shropshire with a specialised library tracing the history of shoes or the **British Institute of Management** in Corby. Not everything is London based, however much the media may try to promote this idea!

Subscription libraries
What else might you find? One rather odd hangover from a long time ago are the subscription libraries. The **London Library** in St. James's Square is probably the most famous of these but at one time every town of any size would have its own library for which the members paid a subscription. The London one survived as did the **Leeds Library** and these now have valuable collections stretching back a long way. Scholars and researchers make a lot of use of these collections.

Languages
If your subject is languages you may find useful help and good libraries in the bodies set up by other countries to promote their language and culture. Examples of these are the **Institut Français du Royaume-Uni** in London which runs a whole programme of classes, films, materials, and a library — all available either free or at a modest charge. The **Goethe Institute** for German also in London, has a similar function.

This chapter has hardly even been the tip of the ice-berg. Libraries exist all over the country for all sorts of people, subjects and reasons.

Some Useful Addresses

Association of Special Libraries
  & Information Bureaux (ASLIB)
3 Belgrave Square
London SW1X 8PL
(01-235-5050)

Association of British Library &
  Information Studies Schools
School of Librarianship
Polytechnic of North London
207-225 Essex Road
London N1 3PN
(01-607 2789)

Book Trust
(formerly National Book League)
Book House
45 East Hill
London SW18 2QZ

British Association of Picture
  Libraries & Agencies
46 Addison Avenue
London W11 4QP
(01-603 8811)

Disabled Living Foundation
380-384 Harrow Road
London W9 2HA

Equal Opportunities Commission
Overseas House
Quay Street
Manchester M3 3HN

Institute of Information Scientists
44 Museum Street
London WC1A 1LY

Library Association
7 Ridgmount Street
London WC1E 7AE
(01-636 7543)

Library Association of Ireland
Thomas Prior House
Merrian Road
Dublin 4

London Library
14 St James's Square
London SW1Y 4LG

Museums Association
34 Bloomsbury Way
London EC1 2SF

Open University
Walton Hall
Milton Keynes
Bucks MK7 6AA
(0908-74066)

Private Libraries Association
Rowelston
South View Road
Pinner
Middx

School Library Association
Liden Library
Barrington Close
Liden
Swindon
Wilts SN3 6HF
(0793-617838)

Scottish Library Association
Department of Librarianship
University of Strathclyde
Livingstone Tower
Richmond Street
Glasgow G1 1XH

● *Tip* Keep looking: the chances are that you will find just what you need.

Reading List

This is a very short list of other books which you may find useful. They all deal, in one way or another, with how to get the best out of the effort you put into your work and may give you some more useful tips.

Acres, D., *How to Pass Exams Without Anxiety*, Northcote House 1987.
Buzan, T., *Use your head*, BBC.
Casey, F., *How to Study: A Practical Guide*, Macmillan 1985.
Cocker, D., *Successful Exam Technique*, Northcote House 1987.
Harrison, C. & Swatridge, C., *Study Sixteen* Oliver and Boyd 1984.
Pain, H., *Where to Join: A Guide for Young People*, Northcote House 1987.
Maddox, H. & Palmer, R., *How to Study*, Pan.
Pope, C., *Brain Train*, E. & F. N. Spon 1984.
Parsons, C., *How to Study Effectively*, Arrow Books 1976.
Sullivan, T., *Studying*, National Extension College 1976.

Glossary

Abstract Usually two or three sentences which contain the main ideas in an article. It can often save you the time and trouble in reading all through the original document.

Archive and archivist An archive is a collection of usually very old historical papers, often the original hand-written documents, and an archivist is the person specially trained not only to look after these fragile papers but also in interpreting them and reading the old writing.

Bar code The succession of black lines often seen on tins and packets in supermarkets but also on the labels of some library books. Running a light pen across these lines transfers the information automatically. There is a barcode on the back cover of this book.

Bibliography A list of books or periodicals. These may be all on the same topic or perhaps published in the same year.

Branch library Large cities or spread-out rural areas will always have one large 'central' library but then all the other areas will be served by separate 'branch' libraries all linked to the main central library.

British Library The title used to describe all the great national libraries which are now banded together as The British Library. Included are such libraries as the British Museum Library and the Science Reference Library.

Bulletin Usually a fairly short newsletter or journal dealing with a specific subject. Its object is to keep all the interested people up-to-date with the latest news.

Catalogue A complete record of all the materials in a library. It may be on cards, on computer (or even in a scrappy exercise book!).

Cataloguing in Publication data A service which has two main prongs. Librarians and booksellers can have advance notice of all the details of a new book about two months before it is published, by this arrangement. The information is then printed on the book so a library can save on its own cataloguing costs by just copying the catalogue entry in the book. (See the front of this book as an example).

Glossary

Ceefax The BBC's Teletext transmissions when they show written information on the screen. If you have a specially adapted set and a remote control you can literally 'turn' the pages and choose what information you want to read. See also **Oracle**.

Chartered Librarian Someone who has completed the courses of study as demanded by the Library Association and passed all the exams, and done a period of work in a library. After all this, you are considered to be a Chartered Librarian. Students now spend at least three years on a degree course followed by work experience.

Classification Putting items together according to some pattern or category. In a library it means the scheme used to decide how to arrange the non-fiction books on the shelves.

Computer search Using a computer terminal which is linked to a telepone to find information from a database held on computer.

Copyright The exclusive ownership granted to the writer of a book or article for a certain number of years. This means that it is against the law to photocopy books and lots of other things like music. However, certain exceptions are made for educational purposes but make sure you check the rules before copying any author's work. The rules are very complicated: ask your librarian.

Copyright deposit library There are a few libraries in the United Kingdom, mostly either large national libraries like the British Library or the Libraries of Oxford and Cambridge Universities, which are given, by law, one copy of every book published in the UK. This dates back to a law passed in 1709.

Database A collection, usually very large, of information. This can be on cards, in a book or in any other format although nowadays it is nearly always taken to mean one held on computer and on a specific subject.

Dewey system A classification system for libraries devised by Melvil Dewey and used very widely all over the world.

Directory These types of books are usually arranged in alphabetical order and are designed as guides, perhaps to who lives in an area (like the telephone directories) or perhaps to all the people in a profession (like The *Library Association Year Book* which is a list of all the members).

Edition Many books, particularly those dealing with a technical subject, may be frequently updated. It may be important to you to know which edition you are reading so always check the title page of the book and, if you are in any doubt, look on the back of the title page and you will find the date of publication of your book.

Glossary

Editor The person in overall control of a publication or series of publications. Newspapers always have an 'editor' but so do most books. This person is responsible for ironing out any problems in the author's writing. Sometimes a book will have contributions from a number of different people and then you will nearly always see an editor's name mentioned as being the organiser of all the material.

Encyclopaedia A book, or set of books, dealing with either just one topic or subject, or (like *Britannica*) with all knowledge. They are arranged alphabetically and are meant to answer queries fairly quickly.

Facsimile A reproduction, usually of the same size, of an original document.

FLA A Fellow of the Library Association is the highest qualification awarded by the Library Association.

Gazeteer A list, usually alphabetical, of places. This is often found at the end of an atlas but it may sometimes be published separately.

HMSO Her Majesty's Stationery Office — in other words the publishing house for all Government publications.

Index An alphabetical list at the back of a book giving you page numbers to the topics you want in that book. This word can also be used to describe the special periodical indexes which are useful if you are doing a literature search.

Information retrieval Ways of both organising material so it can be readily found again and the actual process of searching for it.

Information Science This is now a profession in its own right and concentrates largely on the more technical, *i.e.* computer, methods of both information storage and retrieval. Many information scientists work in industry and specialised libraries dealing with technical subjects.

Inter-Library Loan Scheme Because no library can possibly afford to buy everything, schemes have been set up to allow libraries to borrow books from each other if a borrower requests something they do not have in stock.

Interactive video A video which can respond to the viewer's actions. For example, a video teaching an engineering topic can change its image if the student makes the wrong decision. Some screens are operated by touching them but others have a remote control device. These videos are very useful for training in technical subjects.

Glossary

ISBN The International Standard Book Number, used worldwide to give a unique number to every book published anywhere. It not only identifies the specific book but also which edition it is.

Library Association The professional association for all librarians.

Library of Congress The United States National Library in Washington.

Light pen The special pen used to draw over the bar codes in library books.

Microfiche A way of reducing books and periodicals onto very small pieces of film. These take very little room to store and can be read at a normal print size by putting the microfiche into special machines which have a screen a little like a TV screen.

Oracle The ITV equivalent of Ceefax.

Oversize books Books come in all sorts of shapes and sizes and librarians often have problems in shelving them. To overcome this, many libraries have specially large shelves to house the bigger books. Always remember to check these shelves for anything you want.

Periodical publications Publications that come out in 'parts' over a period of time. Mostly the term refers to magazines and periodicals but it can also mean year-books that appear in a new edition each year.

Prestel This is the Telecom Viewdata service which anyone can use if they have both a specially adapted TV and a telephone linked to it. All sorts of information is available through this service and many firms use it for their own specialised needs (the Travel industry have their own private network on it). Some of the information you have to pay for so it is often only a business or large school or college that will have this service.

Reference Library A library (or department) where you will find books of study, not recreational reading. All the big and expensive encyclopaedias will be kept here. You will usually not be allowed to borrow from a reference library although it should have places for you to sit and study.

Series Usually a group of books with either a related subject (or perhaps for a particular children's age-range) which have a special 'series title'. Sometimes the individual books in a series are numbered.

Study carrel A small booth with a work surface and often an individual light and book-shelf provided for private study in a library. These are sometimes equipped with the necessary machinery to play tapes or watch videos.

VDU Visual Display Unit, as used with computers.

Volume Usually one book in a set, or one year of a magazine or periodical.

Index

abstracts, 48
art collections, 17
art galleries, 51
atlases, 41

bibliographies, 51-52
branch library, 9
British Library, 12, 85-86

careers office, 10
CAL, 74
cassettes, 65
catalogue, 20-21
Ceefax, 73
charitable organisations, 87
children's library, 16
choir sets, 62
church records, 58
Citizen's Advice Bureau, 59
classification, 22
college libraries, 10
commercial library, 17
company records, 59
computer assisted learning, *see* CAL
computer programs, 65
computers, 67-72
computer search, 14, 68-72

databases, 67-72
Dewey Decimal Classification, 22
dictionaries, 39
directories, 40
distance learning, 66

electors' list, 61
encyclopaedias, 38
examination papers, 65
exhibition collections, 63

firms' libraries, 10
folk museums, 54
foreign language books, 64

gazeteers, 41
government libraries, 86-87

government publications, 17

handbooks, 41
hospital libraries, 11

indexes, 48
industrial libraries, 88
industrial museums, 54
information retrieval, 67
interloan, 12

large print books, 63
lending library, 16
Librarians, Professional, 15
libraries, *see* under type of library, eg hospital
Library Assistants, 15
library guides, 24
literature search, 49
local history collections, 63

maps, 64
memory training, 31
mobile library, 9
microfiche, 21
museums, 53-55 *see* also under specific names, eg folk museum
music libraries, 62

National Libraries, 12, 85-86
newspapers, 11, 17, 56
note-taking, 28-30

official leaflets, 62
Open University, 68
Oracle, 73
oversize, 23

patents, 63
periodical lists, 24
periodicals, 17, 46, 47
photocopying, 65
picture libraries, 57
play sets, 62

polytechnic libraries, 10
press cuttings, 57
Prestel, 73
projects, planning, 32, 33, 35
public libraries, 9, 16

reading lists, 24, 51
reading techniques, 26-28
record libraries, 62
record offices, 58
reference books, 37
reference library, 16
research associations, 87
research establishments, 11

scanning, 26-28
school libraries, 10
serendipity, 70
skimming, 28
societies, 11
special needs, 17, 63
studying, 25
subscription libraries, 88

tapes, 65
technical library, 17
teenage library, 64
telephone directories, 40, 61
television, 72-73
time-tabling, 33-35
tourist information, 62

university libraries, 10

video, 62, 65
video, interactive, 74
viewdata, 73

yearbooks, 40

ALSO AVAILABLE

The School Library

Elizabeth King MA ALA

A new discussion of how school libraries are coping in a fast-changing world—a world in which a combination of new ideas, new technology, new management requirements and perennial funding problems present a special challenge for the professional. Practical and readable. Elizabeth King is a past Chairman of the School Library Association and member of the Library Association Joint Board for the Certificate in School Library Studies. 'A stimulating appraisal of the role of the school library in a changing educational world.' *Junior & Middle School Education Journal.* 'A masterly account is given of how to organise a school library... Anyone reading this book will feel invigorated and determined to carry on with the battle of ensuring that all schoolchildren have access to a working school library resource centre.' *School Library Association.*

Where to Join

A Guide for Young People

Helen Pain MLS ALA MIInfSc MBIM

100s of study and leisure ideas for youngsters aged 9 to 16. 'A highly useful starting point for active youngsters... This informative directory will be welcomed by librarians, teachers and young people alike; it provides information succinctly which has not previously been available in collected form.' *Youth Libraries Group News.* 'Has adapted a good idea extremely well.' *Junior Bookshelf.*

How to Survive at College

David Acres BSc(Econ)

The ultimate self-help handbook for students. 'A useful guide... Mr Acres' experience as a student counsellor has given him a very good idea of how students approach their new lifestyle and the range of problems they face.' *Times Higher Education Supplement.*

Northcote House Publishers Ltd, Estover Road, Plymouth PL6 7PZ.